A GREAT IDEA AT THE TIME

ALSO BY ALEX BEAM

Gracefully Insane: Life and Death
Inside America's Premier Mental Hospital

Fellow Travelers

The Americans Are Coming!

A GREAT IDEA AT THE TIME

The Rise, Fall, and Curious Afterlife
of the Great Books

ALEX BEAM

PublicAffairs • New York

Published in the United States by PublicAffairs™,
a member of the Perseus Books Group.

PublicAffairs books are available at special discounts for bulk purchases in the
U.S. by corporations, institutions, and other organizations. For more information, please contact the Special Markets Department at the Perseus Books
Group, 2300 Chestnut Street, Suite 200, Philadelphia, PA 19103, call (800)
810-4145, ext. 5000, or e-mail special.markets@perseusbooks.com.

Designed by Pauline Brown
Text set in 11 point Caslon

Library of Congress Cataloging-in-Publication Data

Beam, Alex.
    A great idea at the time : the rise, fall, and curious afterlife of the Great
Books / Alex Beam.
        p.   cm.
    Includes bibliographical references and index.
    ISBN 978-1-58648-487-3 (alk. paper)
    1. United States—Intellectual life—20th century. 2. Great books of the
Western world. 3. Canon (Literature)—History and criticism. 4. Popular
culture—United States—History—20th century. 5. Books and reading—
Social aspects—United States—History—20th century. 6. Books and
reading—Economic aspects—United States—History—20th century.
7. Education, Humanistic—Social aspects—United States—History—20th
century. I. Title.
    E169.12.B333 2008
    973.91—dc22

                                                            2008033115

First Edition

10 9 8 7 6 5 4 3 2 1

To my three great sons

CONTENTS

INTRODUCTION

O N APRIL 15, 1952, the University of Chicago and the *Encyclopedia Britannica* formally launched the Great Books of the Western World. Millions of Americans had just filed their taxes. It was the night of the New Jersey primary; General Dwight D. Eisenhower, who happened to be in Brussels, had defeated "Mr. Republican," Senator Robert Taft. The very same day, Adlai Stevenson, who would eventually lose to Eisenhower in November, announced he had no intention of running for president.

But at the black-tie gala dinner in the Jade Room of the Waldorf-Astoria Hotel, the subject was not the moment; it was eternity. As the moneyed glitterati of the American mid-century— the Rockefellers, the Goodriches, the Houghtons, and the Vanderbilts—feasted on prime rib of beef, they were invited to cast their eyes upward to a raised dais. There sat a freshly minted set of the deluxe, faux-leather Great Books, all fifty-four volumes of them, nine years in the making, stuffed with 443 works by seventy four white male authors, purporting to encompass all of Western knowledge from Homer to Freud. Great Britain's consul general, H. A. Hobson, was on hand, prepared, in theory, to pass the first Great Books set on to his boss, Queen Elizabeth. A few months later, in a similarly staged event, President Harry S Truman would receive his Great Books at the White House.

The star of the show was Robert Maynard Hutchins, the glamorous, no longer young, former president of the University of Chicago, who had published the books with his brilliant, Hobbit-like sidekick, Mortimer Adler. Hutchins, the "boy wonder" appointee to the Chicago presidency in 1929, had left the Hyde Park campus the year before. Hutchins's Yale classmate and boon companion, William Benton, ad man and hustler extraordinaire, took the podium to pronounce the Great Books project "the most significant publishing event since Dr. Johnson's dictionary." Hutchins himself looked upon his work and declared it to be good: "Great Books of the Western World is an act of piety," he proclaimed. "Here are the sources of our being."

Make no mistake: This was no charitable act of cultural enrichment. Hutchins, Adler, and Benton had wallpapered their launch event with pseudo-celebrities and rich people for one purpose only, to sell sets of what Hutchins sardonically called their "colorful furniture." They were taking a big risk. They had bet $2 million on the proposition that an American family would repair to the den after dinner and crack open Christian Huygens's 1690 *Treatise on Light*, chock-full of forbidding, spiderweb diagrams, or mull over this excerpt from chapter 5, "On the Strange Refractions of Iceland Crystal": "For we have stated before this that the line N being the radius of a spherical wave of light in air, while in the crystal it spread through the spheroid ABPS, the ration of N to CS will be 156,962 to 93,410."

The books were full of speed bumps. Yes, there was Shakespeare, as well as Tolstoy's *War and Peace* (no *Anna Karenina;* too readable!). But there was also Ptolemy's endless Tables of Anom-

William Benton, Robert Hutchins, and Mortimer Adler celebrate "the most significant publishing event since Dr. Johnson's dictionary."
DEPARTMENT OF SPECIAL COLLECTIONS, UNIVERSITY OF CHICAGO

alies for the apogees of the planetary orbits in specific skies; Copernicus's charts of the parallaxes and semidiameters of our solar system; and, in musical notation, Johannes Kepler's cosmic question, "In the Celestial Harmonies Which Planet Sings Soprano, Which Alto, Which Tenor, and Which Bass?"

The Great Books of the Western World were in fact icons of unreadability—32,000 pages of tiny, double-column, eye-straining type. There were no concessions to contemporary taste, or even pleasure. The translations of the great works were not particularly modern. There were no footnotes to mitigate the reader's ignorance, or gratify his curiosity. Only two nominal twentieth-century writers, William James and Sigmund Freud, made the cut. No Romantic poets, no Mark Twain, and no Jane Austen. Yet backed by advertising hype and by unscrupulous, foot-in-the-door salesmen, Britannica would eventually sell 1 million sets, each costing several hundred dollars each. Against all odds, the Great Books joined the roster of postwar fads like drive-ins, hula hoops, and Mexican jumping beans. Tens of thousands of Americans rushed to join Great Books discussion groups, prompting *Time* magazine to print the hilarious claim that "Great Books has switched many Americans—at least temporarily—from the works of Spillane to those of Spinoza and St. Augustine."

And then, nothing.

Well, almost nothing. Sales sputtered in the late 1960s, flat-lined in the 1970s, and later fell off the cliff. An attempted 1990 relaunch of the Great Books—this time with women!—was a disaster. Unsold sets of the Great Books of the Western World now languish in a warehouse. Britannica no longer markets them. Among major universities, only Columbia, where the whole idea began, still force-feeds a much-abbreviated version of the Great Books curriculum to its undergraduates. Tiny St. John's College, created by disciples of Hutchins and Adler, still devotes all four years to teaching the Great Books, as Hutchins vainly hoped the University of Chicago would do. In the late 1940s, Hutchins predicted that 15 million Americans would eventually join Great Books discussion groups. The Great Books Foundation, which ekes out an existence in Chicago's ornate, riverfront Jewelry Building, optimistically estimates that 10,000 Americans now participate in their discussion groups.

What's astonishing is not that the number is so small but that any groups exist at all. "We are a dying breed," admits Carol

Beam, not a relation, who hosts an annual Great Books week at Colby College in Maine. "It's sort of an underground thing now."

Underground, indeed. I had never heard of the Great Books until a reader of my column in the *Boston Globe* sent me an e-mail asking why a company called Liberal Arts, Inc., bought a huge estate in Stockbridge, Massachusetts, in 1947. Curious, I learned that millionaire, dilettante, Great Books devotee Paul Mellon was planning to move St. John's College from Annapolis to the Berkshires. (It never happened.) One thing led to another, and suddenly I had plunged myself into the romantic and chaotic world of Hutchins, Adler, and their irrepressible intellectual hucksterism. My ignorance abetted my bliss. Making the acquaintance of Robert Hutchins for the first time, as so many of his colleagues said at the time, was like falling in love. On the other hand, to be reading Mortimer Adler's two autobiographies and watching his endless, self-promotional television appearances was a nightmare from which I am still struggling to awake. To write this book, I joined Carol Beam's "underground," attending Great Books weekends, visiting St. John's College, and walking across the street to my local library for Great Books nights, to discuss Gibbon, Machiavelli, and Aristophanes. I even bought a set of the books, enticed by this too-candid description on eBay:

> You are bidding on a set of 54 volumes of the Encyclopedia Britannica Great Books of the Western World. This set is complete. These are black leatherette hardcovers with gold on the tops of the pages. There are no creases, torn pages, dog ears or damage of any kind. All are beautiful, clean and bright. *I doubt these have ever been opened or read* (emphasis added).

They do crack mightily upon opening.

Who *did* read these books? Who chose them, anyway? Who bought them? Why did the Great Books die? Or did they? Who is still reading them? Did Thomas Aquinas ("a walking wine barrel," G. K. Chesterton called him) really need a donkey cart to move from one place to another? I decided to answer these questions in a brief, engaging, and undidactic history of the Great Books.

A book as different from the ponderous and forbidding Great Books as it could possibly be.

ONE

THE
HEADWATERS

WHERE TO BEGIN? Why not with Frederic William Farrar, the Dean of Canterbury, a former Harrow schoolmaster, friend of Charles Darwin, biographer of Jesus Christ, and ex-Apostle, a member of Cambridge University's most rarefied intellectual club. Farrar wrote a series of essays on Great Books in 1898 for the London monthly *The Sunday Magazine*, hailing five authors as "supreme": Dante, Milton, Bunyan, Thomas à Kempis, and William Shakespeare. Around the same time, the French Positivist philosopher Auguste Comte assembled his Positivist Library, 270 works by about 140 authors, many of whom we might call the usual suspects: Byron, Goethe, Gibbon, and Hume.

In his later years, Comte began to practice what he called "hygiene cerebral," shunning newspapers and other chroniclers of the moment to focus his mind on the eternal verities. Instead of catching up on the news, each morning he would read—presumably for the umpteenth time—a snippet of Dante or part of Kempis's *Imitation of Christ*. He and Farrar agreed that great books chased out the bad, and worse: Time spent with the classics might otherwise be "deplorably wasted in devouring scraps of disconnected and vapid intelligence," Farrar wrote. As Stanford scholar W. B. Carnochan put it:

> The Victorian age was intellectually and spiritually intoxicated by the greatness of great books, comforted by what F. D. Maurice (in the title lecture of a volume published in 1856) called "The Friendship of Books" and Alexander Ireland called the "solace and companionship of books," . . . obsessed with the dangerous proliferation of bad books, and awash in advice never to settle for or to indulge in the second-rate, much less to permit oneself to indulge in a surfeit of journalistic ephemera.

Then and now, the Great Books lent themselves to gimmickry. Another son of Victoria's England, John Lubbock, member of Parliament, amateur scientist, father of eleven children, and principal of the Working Men's College in London, proposed a list of his era's 100 best books and published it in the *Pall Mall Gazette*, a popular illustrated newspaper. There were no particular surprises: Homer and Virgil; Aeschylus and Sophocles; Shakespeare, Milton, and Dante; Bacon, Descartes, and Locke; Thackeray, Dickens, and George Eliot. But unlike subsequent canoneers, Lubbock made no special claims for his list, and indeed encouraged others to suggest changes. Smelling a circulation booster, the *Gazette* sent Lubbock's list and a request for comment to the notables of the day, almost all of whom mailed their emendations back to the paper. A public parlor game was born.

Novelist Wilkie Collins, the headmasters of Eton and Harrow, the American minister to Great Britain, and William Morris all sent in suggested changes. Cardinal Newman politely replied in the third person, saying "he was not up to the task." John Ruskin returned the list, having run his pen through the entries that he considered "rubbish and poison": Mill, Darwin, Adam Smith, Descartes, Berkeley, and Locke. He hated Edward Gibbon, author of *The Decline and Fall of the Roman Empire*, and told the *Gazette* why: "Good men study and wise men describe, only the growth and standing of things, not their decay." What's more, "Gibbon's is the worst English that was ever written by an educated Englishman."

Forgotten novelist James Payn voiced the secret thoughts of many Great Books–sloggers over the years: "When I look through the list of books you send me I cannot help saying to myself, 'Here are the most admirable and varied materials for the formation of a prig.'"

The most famous—and most dubious—response arrived from Edward the Prince of Wales, the future King Edward VII, popularly known as "Edward the Caresser" for pursuing high-profile love affairs with the likes of actress Lillie Langtry and others. In a painfully orotund reply to Lubbock drafted by his secretary ("I am desired by the Prince of Wales to thank you for your letter . . ."), His Royal Highness "venture[d] to remark that the works of Dryden should not be omitted from such an important and comprehensive list." The letter elicited mute guffaws, as Edward maintained a George W. Bush–like distance from the literary affairs of his day.

The next man to take a crack at selecting Great Books was Charles Eliot, the retiring—literally, not figuratively—president of Harvard. Appointed president in 1869, Eliot had cut a broad swath through American education. First, he had started the transformation of Harvard from a gentlemen's college into a modern university by shoring up the law and medical schools, and adding a European-style graduate school in the humanities. Second, he smashed the existing undergraduate curriculum to smithereens. Before Eliot, the young men at Harvard, Yale, and Princeton took pretty much the same courses, for all four years:

Harvard freshman year: Greek, Latin, Math, French, Elocution, Ethics

Yale freshman year: Greek, Latin, Math

Harvard sophomore year: Physics; Chemistry; German; recite twenty chapters of Gibbon; Greek; Latin; Math

Yale sophomore year: Greek, Latin, Math

Harvard junior year: Philosophy, Physics, Chemistry, Forensics

Yale junior year: Greek, Math, Logic, Physics, Rhetoric

Harvard senior year: History, Philosophy, Latin, Greek

Yale senior year: Philosophy, Moral and Mental; Chemistry; Geology; Political Science; History; Rhetoric

Those were, respectively, the Harvard curriculum of 1869 and Yale's of 1875. Yale's official historian, George Pierson, called the pedagogy "moribund." It was a grind, pure and simple, with students parroting back lines from obscure Greek poems or dozing through lecture cycles by superannuated profs. "The emphasis on memorizing and repeating made automatons of the tutors and disciplinarians of the professors," Pierson wrote. At Harvard, Princeton, or Yale, "[a] medieval schoolman would at once have known where he was," Pierson continued: smack in the heart of the ancient curricula, the Trivium—grammar, rhetoric, and logic—and the Quadrivium—arithmetic, geometry, astronomy, and music. The first two and a half years of the elite Ivy League education dated back a thousand years!

Despite a public plea from his fellow university presidents, Eliot jettisoned Harvard's Greek requirement in 1884, and by 1899 the college had an all-elective curriculum. Yale grudgingly followed suit, introducing "optional" courses into the four-year-long course of study. Eliot "firmly believed that a young man of eighteen or nineteen could choose his course, even among infinite combinations, better than anyone else could do it for him," according to Harvard historian Samuel Eliot Morison. By the beginning of the new century, Morison noted, the college catalog fat with elective course offerings "seemed to be as firmly established as the trivium and quadrivium of the middle ages." He compared the modern course list to the fat Sears Roebuck catalogs emanating from the company's headquarters in Chicago. Just a few years after Eliot had implemented his reforms, Sears opened a $5 million, 3-million-square-foot mail-order fulfillment building, on Chicago's West Side, the largest business building in the world. America was becoming a land of consumers, and a land of choice. Chemistry professor Charles Eliot was very much in tune with the times.

Eliot's reform casts a long shadow on the events of this book. Robert Maynard Hutchins graduated from Yale in 1921 and later claimed he had learned next to nothing in New Haven. During his twenty-year tenure as president of the University of Chicago, he dreamed of instituting a four-year, required undergraduate curriculum modeled on the medieval Quadrivium and Trivium. Hutchins hated what Eliot had done. "He thought President Eliot was the greatest educational criminal ever born," former University of Chicago president Hannah Gray told me, "because he championed the elective system." Curiously, both Eliot and Hutchins despised undergraduate football, and one of Eliot's few failures during his forty-year reign was his repeated failure to ban the sport, which he called "more brutalizing than prize-fighting, cock-fighting, or bull-fighting."

But Eliot's schedule-jiggering pedagogy had little to do with his championing of the first American set of "great books," the Harvard Classics. In the final year of his Harvard presidency, he casually mentioned in a speech to a working-class audience that a five-foot shelf of books would provide "a good substitute for a liberal education in youth to anyone who would read them with devotion, even if he could spare but fifteen minutes a day for reading." Of course, that was precisely the kind of education he had just eliminated in Cambridge. Two editors from P. F. Collier's publishing house challenged Eliot to follow through on his comment, and the Harvard Classics were born. It wasn't much more than a publicity stunt, albeit a very successful and lucrative one, for both Harvard and Collier.

What did Eliot include in his portable university? Two volumes of Darwin, Adam Smith, a smattering of Copernicus and Newton, and Dante and Shakespeare of course. In a 2001 article in *Harvard* magazine, critic Adam Kirsch noted that Eliot, a man of science, mistrusted his instincts, which were poor, on questions of imaginative literature. He liked *The Odyssey* but not *The Iliad*, and included the poetry of Robert Burns but not that of Chaucer. Kirsch ascribed to Eliot "a settled distrust of abstract thought; in every case, Eliot prefers autobiography to speculation." Astonishingly, Eliot chose not to include Aristotle or Thomas Aquinas. He likewise cold-shouldered Nietzsche, Marx, and Freud. "There is something obviously flawed about a criterion that admits Richard Henry Dana's moderately interesting memoir 'Two Years Before the Mast,' because it is 'fact,' but has no place for 'Moby Dick' because it is 'fiction,'" Kirsch wrote. A cynic might attribute Dana's inclusion to his Harvard education—he also taught there—while Melville, who left school to become a cabin boy, memorably wrote that "a whale-ship was my Yale College and my Harvard."*

But here is the point: The Harvard Classics made a lot of money. The admen didn't shy away from hucksterism (e.g., "How to Get Rid of an Inferiority Complex")—buy the five-foot shelf! Collier sold 350,000 sets of the Classics in twenty years. Those are not *Gone with the Wind*–type numbers, but they are not bad for challenging reading.

In 1916, the Harvard Classics caught the eye of a precocious 15-year-old in Washington Heights, Manhattan, who had quit high school to work at a daily newspaper, the *New York Sun*. In a nighttime extension class offered by Columbia University, young Mortimer Adler bumped up against the *Autobiography* of John Stuart Mill, who could read Greek at 3 and by age 5 was conversant with Plato's dialogues. Throw me in that briar patch, was Adler's age-inappropriate reaction. In search of Plato, Adler looked in on his neighbor, one Sam Feldman, a lawyer and inveterate book buyer, who owned Mr. Eliot's famous shelf. Adler quickly devoured four of Plato's dialogues and became "so fascinated by the Socratic method of questioning that I persuaded my friends to engage in mock dialogues." "I have it on the testimony of my sister that I was a difficult child," he recalled.

The young Adler, who would later trumpet the superiority of his and Hutchins's 62-inch shelf, the Great Books of the Western

---

* After printing Kirsch's article about the Classics, the editors at *Harvard* magazine pulled a *Pall Mall Gazette:* They invited their readers to submit their own lists of great books for a hypothetical new edition. The suggestions ranged from *Feminism and Art History*, by Norma Broude and Mary Garrardbook, to Hunter Thompson's *Fear and Loathing in Las Vegas*. The two books most often chosen were Richard Feynman's *Lectures on Physics* and James Joyce's *Ulysses*. ("A monument of Irish wit," Robert Hutchins called it when he helped choose Chicago's 1952 Great Books, "but I am not sure that justifies its inclusion." It didn't.) Neither Joyce nor Feynman appeared in the 1990 revised and "modernized" edition of Chicago's Great Books.

World, to Mr. Eliot's paltry 60 inches, proclaimed himself "dissatisfied with the incompleteness of the selections from Plato." "I bought a secondhand set of the Jowett translations in five volumes and began to spend time at my desk at the 'Sun' reading the dialogues of Plato instead of doing the work that earned my weekly paycheck," he later wrote.

Comes now John Erskine, a professor in the early-twentieth-century Ivy League mold, son of a well-to-do New Jersey factory owner, whose acolytes later called him the "spiritual father" or "onlie begetter" of the Great Books. Although Erskine indeed begat many of the events described in this book, paternity of the Great Books movement was only one chapter in his very unusual life. An expert on Elizabethan poetry, Erskine was also a gifted pianist who left his Columbia University sinecure in 1927 to become the first president of the reorganized Juilliard School of Music, which had merged with the Institute of Music Art. And although he bears much responsibility for tormenting successive generations of Columbia undergraduates with required "core curriculum" classes devoted to Herodotus, Thucydides, Montaigne, and Boccacio, Erskine himself wrote for a much broader audience. Starting with his breezy, inane, best-selling novel, *The Private Life of Helen of Troy*, his popular novels, loosely grounded in the classics, graced many a national best-seller list.

A gentleman of the old school—he was a vestryman at the 92nd Street Trinity Episcopal parish, where he rubbed shoulders with the Columbia trustees—Erskine was refreshingly free of hang-ups. He knew a great book when he saw one. "A great book is one that has meaning, and continues to have meaning, for a variety of people over a long period of time," he proclaimed, and he knew that he wanted to teach such books to undergraduates.

Erskine had been a Columbia undergrad himself, and he shared the campus sentiment that his students were reading less good literature than their fathers had. In 1916, the University's Committee on Instruction fretted that the electives curriculum, aping Harvard, was eroding the "social aspect of scholarship," inasmuch as students were wandering off in all directions. Furthermore, the Committee noted that the typical Columbia student "is said not to know the great authors in polite literature; he is said not to know what has happened in the world; and he is said not to know the master ideas in philosophy and science." They compared this hypothetical student unfavorably with "the superlatively educated college man of only a generation or so ago, who was on speaking terms with the classics in the fields of literature, of history, of philosophy. . . ."

Erskine, like Robert Hutchins after him, felt it was "the elective system within American education that had contributed to the students' lack of familiarity [with 'great' authors and] to an inability to talk about them," according to Great Books historian Hugh Moorhead. "College students, he noticed,"

> could no longer hold conversations with their fellow classmates on anything held in common other than one or two textbooks. . . . In Erskine's own college days, at the beginning of the century, everyone took the same courses, had the same books, many of them great. . . . Both good literature and good conversation, the two complementing one another, flourished.

Just before proposing a great-books course to the Columbia faculty in 1917, Erskine accepted an assignment to join the American Expeditionary Force in France as an educational adviser, first to the YMCA, and then to the U.S. Army. At General John Pershing's request, Erskine opened a huge, temporary university for

12,000 American soldiers waiting to return from France after World War I. Pershing worried that his doughboys, freed from the trenches, might wreak havoc on the French countryside. "All they need is something to occupy their minds," Pershing told Erskine. "Keep their minds busy, or they'll concentrate on girls and cognac. Then there'll be street fights, and France will want to throw us out."

Erskine's university at Beaune offered courses in history, English, geometry, arithmetic, bookkeeping, commercial law, foreign trade, principles of accounting, shorthand, agriculture, engineering, heating and ventilation, and automobile mechanics— anything that might appeal to a demobilized soldier. Erskine loved the job—"If you were here for five minutes, you would see that this work is the moral and intellectual salvation of thousands of boys," he wrote his mother—and he loved the idea that Beaune had no academic departments and no degree requirements, unlike its stateside equivalents. "When you apply at the door of a university for instruction in a particular thing," he told his soldiers in 1919, "you find that the university expects you to become a candidate for a degree. . . . [I]t expects to label you." And he was perfectly happy to have grown-ups in the classroom. "The education of adults ought to be as natural in society as the education of youth," he wrote.

Back at Columbia, Erskine again pitched his great-books course idea for the 1920 academic year. "Why not treat *The Iliad*, *The Odyssey*, and other masterpieces as though they were recent publications, calling for immediate investigation and discussion?" he proposed, pointing out that most classics were shorter than contemporary novels and had been written for broad audiences in their time.

I was told that reading Homer in translation would be the same thing as not reading Homer at all. . . . I couldn't help adding that I marveled at my colleagues who did their reading exclusively in the original. I publicly offered them my sympathy for never having read the Old Testament, nor the words of Christ. Of course the Old Testament was possible for any colleague who knew Hebrew, but there was no text extant of the words of Christ in the language he spoke.

"The faculty rejoinders were rather warm" was Erskine's genteel way of saying that the German Department didn't want Goethe to be studied in English, the Latin Department felt *The Aeneid* was unreachable in translation, and so on down the line. One faculty member wrote a letter complaining that the proposed two-year-long General Honors course, which would devote a single two-hour seminar to one work each week, would prove too difficult for the typical Columbia College man: "When is he to eat and sleep? How much real grasp will he get of any of these authors?" Erskine's plan "will be most unfortunate for *true* scholarship in Columbia College," this anonymous faculty member wrote:

> If that institution is to make a choice, it should stand for *exact knowledge of a few things rather than for superficial acquaintance with many things*. I firmly believe that it is better that a man should get to *know ten authors well* in his last two years in college, than that he should learn *the names of the eighty-four men* presented to him on this list (emphasis in original).

Eventually, "worn out by futile talk," as Erskine put it, the exasperated faculty allowed him to proceed.

Erskine adopted a formula for teaching the Great Books that is still used today. Two teachers sat in a classroom with about twenty or twenty-five students and launched a discussion, Socratic style. The teachers were "selected for their disposition to disagree with each other," Erskine recalled in his 1948 memoir, *My Life as a Teacher*. A typical question used to launch the two-hour discussion might have been: "What is the ruling passion in *The Iliad*?" Erskine didn't require his assistants to be experts on *The Song of Roland* or the Federalist Papers; he merely wanted them to be smart, and to have read the book. The conventional baggage of literary criticism—biographical details, the historical context— was excluded from the classroom. Just the text, mister, two hours of it, with only one short break.

Mortimer Adler, who had enrolled in General Honors as a Columbia junior in 1921, started teaching the course as a graduate student in 1923. He and his coteacher Mark Van Doren taught "like debonair amateurs," Adler later wrote, "assured that even if the book under consideration was difficult . . . we at least should be able to read it better than our students."

At least most of the time. In his memoirs, Adler recalled that the first year he taught the class, he overprepared and lectured the young men instead of provoking discussion. One especially brilliant student "took the class away from me any time he wanted by asking better questions or interjecting more sophisticated comments." Exasperated, Adler bumped into the man on campus one day and confessed his feelings of inadequacy. "Would you like me to help you teach the seminar?" Clifton Fadiman asked. Fadiman later became the book editor of the *New Yorker*, editor in chief at Simon & Schuster, a lifelong friend of Adler's, and an inveterate "Great Bookie."

Adler's coteacher Van Doren also became a lifelong friend, a renowned Columbia professor, a prolific anthologist and tastemaker like Fadiman, and a Pulitzer Prize–winning poet. Their correspondence was extraordinarily affectionate; Adler named his first son after Van Doren. Another General Honors teacher, Rexford Tugwell, became a member of Franklin Roosevelt's "brain trust" and headed FDR's Depression-era resettlement administration. Adler's class also included Lionel Trilling, who became a popular and accomplished English professor at Columbia. Trilling and his equally famous colleague Jacques Barzun taught a version of General Honors, rechristened the Colloquium on Important Books, for thirty years.

In its eighty-eight-year history, General Honors has been abandoned, renamed, relentlessly retooled, and then twinned with a Classical Civilization curriculum also introduced at Columbia in 1920. Erskine's class exists to this day. LitHum, or Literature and the Humanities, and CC, Classical Civilization, are still taught in two-hour-long sessions in Hamilton Hall, right where Erskine first addressed his first class.

The history of the Great Books proceeds on two tracks: college courses and adult education. The first formal Great Books courses for adults were held at the People's Institute, which operated out of Cooper Union for the Advancement of Science and Art on Manhattan's Union Square. Founded in 1897, the Institute mainly sponsored lecture series and discussion groups on the burning issues of the day. Typically, it offered three lectures a week, sometimes attracting audiences of over a thousand to Cooper's cavernous Great Hall. Anyone could and did show up:

bums, lawyers, businessmen, and students. With speeches devoted to communism, pacifism, and atheism, conflict was inevitable. When a biologist delivered a stirring defense of vivisectionism, cutting up animals for medical research, a near riot ensued, and the police had to be summoned. It was not unheard of for an audience member to wake up in the middle of a lecture, mount the stage, and deliver competing remarks from the same platform.

In 1926, a newly hired staff assistant, Scott Buchanan, knew the Institute wanted to broaden its offerings; the Carnegie Corporation was increasing its funding from $2,500 to $10,000 a year. His friend, the 24-year-old Mortimer Adler, had a suggestion: Why not offer the Columbia General Honors program to a public audience?

Erskine, who had not only taught adults at the upstate New York Chautauqua Institute but had also run a mini-university at Beaune, wasn't interested. Van Doren had also taught Chautauqua courses, yet he, too, declined. But Adler was "on fire" with the idea, Buchanan later recalled, and together with Institute director Everett Dean Martin, they got Carnegie on board. Adler and his Columbia colleagues would offer two courses on the History of Thought, one Classic and Medieval, the other Renaissance and Modern. The first year attracted 134 students, broken into six groups, with two discussion leaders, just as they were conducted on the Columbia campus at Morningside Heights. The groups met in churches, YMCAs, settlement houses, and sometimes in the instructors' homes. The courses were free, but students were warned that they would have to pay between ten cents and a dollar for each of the twenty books on the syllabus, if they couldn't find them in a library.

Adler and Whittaker Chambers—yes, *that* Whittaker Chambers—team-taught a class on "Renaissance and Modern

Thought" at the Community Church on East 34th Street. In order to get paid, Adler had to submit a "Leader's Class Report," and his handwritten weekly summaries are now in an archive at the New York Public Library.

In November 1926, Adler reported that his group was

1. lively in discussion

2. full of prejudices and "ideas"

3. likely to read

4. "shockable"

5. untrained intellectually and needs *dialectic* therefore

In December, following a session on Descartes, Adler recorded that "[t]he discussion of Descartes was better than I expected. They were most interested in God and his existence." Following a Shakespeare class, he wrote that his Institute-niks were "as good as my Columbia groups." High praise indeed.

Fadiman and Richard McKeon, who would later become a dean at the University of Chicago, taught "Classic and Medieval Thought" at the West Side YMCA on West 5th Street. "Recalling that Socrates had taught in the market place," Fadiman wrote in his essay collection *Party of One*,

> [w]e saw nothing wrong in continuing our discussion over cafeteria tables. Our students were wildly random. Merchant mariners marooned until the next voyage. . . . Brash dogmatists who had read Marx and didn't want to understand anything else. Pale-faced Emersonian clergymen. Young stenographers, their eyes reflecting the solitude of the dismal hall bedroom.

Comfortable matrons pouncing on a bargain in culture. Professional arguers trailing their soap boxes. Recent immigrants
seeking a key to a bewildering America. Those too poor to go
to college. Those thirsty for something college had been too
poor to give them.

Under the influence of the Great Books, Fadiman wrote, "[t]he
Marxist launched fewer manifestoes. The arguer stepped down
from his soap box. The truck driver grew less arrogant, the immi-
grant less humble." One of his students was a night watchman
who lived on a barge in the East River and did his reading at the
Public Library on 42nd Street. McKeon wished the partially educated bargeman would get a degree, because "he would have been
a better teacher than most of the ones we have in college."

Carnegie viewed the downtown Great Books classes as "experimental," and they lasted for only two academic years,
1926–1927 and 1927–1928. Within just a few years, Adler,
Buchanan, and McKeon would be reunited at the University of
Chicago.

TWO

THE
ODD COUPLE

THERE IS A LOVELY, revealing story of how Mortimer Adler, the son of a Washington Heights jewelry salesman, first met Robert Maynard Hutchins, the refined child of a high-minded Presbyterian clergyman. The year was 1927, and Hutchins was dean of the Yale Law School. Hutchins was turning the law school upside down, democratizing admissions, broadening the course offerings, and rewriting the musty textbooks where necessary. He was personally reworking J. H. Wigmore's classic text on evidence, and learned from a friend that Adler, then a 24-year-old graduate assistant at Columbia, had alluded to the dialectics of legal casuistry in a footnote of his soon-to-be-published book, *Dialectic*. Letters were exchanged. Characteristically, Adler speed-read all five volumes of Wigmore, "with growing puzzlement and consternation," as he wrote to Hutchins: "There is a job of profound logical clarification to be done."

Hutchins invited Adler to visit him in New Haven. Stepping off the train on a muggy August day, Adler was dressed in a black suit and hat. "My experience with deans at Columbia," Adler later recalled, "led me to expect a man of advanced years, portly in appearance, and somberly dressed." Not at all. A young man, only three years older than Adler, answered the door at the dean's office. He had dark, wavy brilliantined hair and stood 6 feet 3 inches tall. In some photographs, he resembled the young, sallow, ladykilling Orson Welles. He was "collar-ad" handsome, with the kind of good looks one saw in magazine advertisements. Black wasn't his color. Hutchins was wearing white tennis trousers, a white T-shirt, and sneakers.

Assuming that one of the learned professor's children had answered the door, Adler stuttered, as he often did when flustered. "I am here to see Mr. Hutchins."

"That's me," replied the vision in white. "Come on in."

And so the Talmudic Terrier met the Boy Wonder.

There are many ways to characterize the unlikely pairing, and the lifelong friendship and collaboration, of Hutchins and Adler: Hutchins as Don Quixote, Adler as Sancho Panza. Hutchins as the patrician WASP whom the low-born Adler held in awe. Adler as the striving, ambitious son desperately seeking to please the laconic, distant father. I find it easier to think of them as two fascinating people, one of whom you would like to be, and one of whom you would not.

One would like to have been Robert Hutchins. Success came easily and early to Hutchins. At least he made it look easy. By the time he met Adler, he was not only dean of a great law school, he had also married a statuesque beauty—an artist, sculptor, and novelist. Maude Hutchins was an aristocratic, enigmatic vamp who dressed only in black and white. Adler, a troll next to the godlike Hutchins, had embarked on what began as a *coup de foudre* love affair with a beautiful Barnard girl he spotted at a Nantucket beach party and later devolved into a loveless marriage of convenience. ("I should have had more sense," he confessed.) Adler was brilliantly book-smart, logorrheic, and endlessly self-absorbed. He wrote not one but two autobiographies, and often added his own works to Great Books reading lists for courses he taught. I was transfixed watching an educational TV show he made in 1953 called "How to Watch Television," an allusion to his best-selling book, *How to Read a Book.* Adler showed mid-century audiences "how to actively watch a television program"—by watching himself on television.

First, Hutchins. His father was indeed a minister, and a very successful one, who taught at Oberlin College and then ran Berea College, a philanthropic, no-tuition school for the penniless children of Appalachia. Robert attended hyperliberal Oberlin (more of a cause than a college, it was said), served as an ambulance driver in World War I, and then entered his father's alma mater, Yale, as a junior. Hutchins was a gifted writer and a charismatic speaker, "a preacher at heart," according to biographer William McNeill. Hutchins broke with his father's religion after leaving home in 1918 and "spent the rest of his life trying to find a substitute for his father's Bible, without ever quite succeeding," McNeill writes.

Hutchins cared enough about religion in later life to remember when and where he swore off churches for good, after hearing a sermon by University of Chicago chaplain Charles Whitney Gilkey in Rockefeller Chapel. The chaplain began his sermon with the familiar chestnut "Yesterday I was on the golf course, and as I teed off I was reminded that we must follow through in life." Something inside of Hutchins snapped. "These were not serious gatherings," he recalled. "They were social assemblies of one kind or another." I would not be the first to point out that proselytizing the classical education contained in the Great Books became a lifelong, quasi-religious crusade for the minister's son from Ohio.

By the time Adler caught up with Hutchins, the winsome dean had crammed a lifetime of accomplishments into twenty-nine short years. Voted most likely to succeed in the Yale class of 1921, he delivered the senior-class oration on the subject "Should Institutions of Learning Be Abolished?" In that speech, he likened Yale to a "convenient country club" that conferred "social graces" upon its undergraduates. Hutchins was a scholarship boy who had to wash dishes to earn his tuition. That put him in a small minority at the blue-blooded Ivy League finishing school, where the prep school hordes called boys who worked their way through college "Arabs" and "Chinese." Hutchins was alert to the social and intellectual entropy of the self-satisfied "college man." In another speech, he took note of Yale's astonishing political homogeneity: Only 7 of 236 graduates of the Sheffield Scientific School identified themselves as Democrats. "Those who grow apprehensive about atheism and Bolshevism in the colleges merely betray their ignorance," he railed, "for the most conservative places in America today, as faculty members know, are the universities."

The young Hutchins once remarked that being a "Yale man" had many benefits, but "these benefits had nothing to do with any intellectual development." The idealism of Oberlin and the cynical sense of entitlement he encountered at Yale made Hutchins a small-"d" democrat for life.

After graduation, Hutchins took a not very promising job at the Lake Placid School in upstate New York, a boarding school of last resort for well-to-do young men who were having trouble passing the College Board entrance exams. On the mistaken assumption that Hutchins was interested in education—he swore he wasn't—Yale president James Angell quickly recalled the newly married graduate back to New Haven to be secretary of the university. Angell mentored Hutchins and allowed him to study for a law degree while working in the administration. With his easy charm and gift for gab—biographer Harry Ashmore writes that Hutchins's many speeches for Yale were touched by "sardonic gaiety"—he addressed dozens of alumni groups, passing the hat for donations. Speaking to the reunion class of 1896, he reminded them of students, such as he, who "had not been born in Pierce Arrow limousines" and urged them to give generously to scholarship funds.

In 1925, Hutchins received his law degree. Within a year, he was the acting dean of the Law School. By 1927 he was the dean, subtly propelled into office with Angell's hand on his back. Hutchins had ideas, and quickly acted on them, or at least tried to. He wanted to make admission to Yale Law based solely on grades, to reduce the number of "gentlemen" finding their way in through family connections. He sought to merge legal studies with the new social sciences, and hoped to add an anthropologist and a psychologist to his faculty. Columbia Law School had just turfed out a like-minded pack of reformers, one of them another scholarship boy, William O. Douglas from Yakima, Washington, whom Hutchins promptly hired and befriended.

Douglas's brusque classroom manner prompted a revolt of his students, who sent a committee to Hutchins demanding the future Supreme Court justice be fired. In his memoir, *Go East, Young Man*, Douglas wrote that

> the students were the grandsons of very eminent and at times disreputable characters, and that as a result of the wealth of their ancestors the students had been spoiled all their lives. I said I thought it was time they learned that when they stood before a court or a jury, they would be judged by their perception and fidelity to the law, not by their ancestors.

"It's fine with me if you fire me," I said.

"Don't be silly. I'm merely passing the complaint on to you," Hutchins told me.

"I am inclined to bear down even harder on the spoiled brats."

"That would be revolutionary and wonderful."

Hutchins was the Golden Boy. Within eighteen months, he was already receiving preliminary feelers about filling the vacant presidency of the University of Chicago. The world of elite uni-

Dreamboat at large: In the inscription to William Benton, Hutchins says he resembles "a retired, second-rate Shakespearean actor gazing into his past."
DEPARTMENT OF SPECIAL COLLECTIONS, UNIVERSITY OF CHICAGO

versities was quite small in 1929. Angell, for instance, had been recruited to teach philosophy at the University of Chicago by John Dewey and remained a professor there for a quarter century. He knew the men on the University of Chicago search committee and confided to them that his fractious, brilliant young colt of a dean probably needed five more years of seasoning before taking over a major research university. They politely ignored his warnings, and Hutchins eventually took the job, partly because he had a problem that was not immediately apparent on first meeting: Robert Hutchins was easily bored.

That had never been Mortimer Adler's problem. He, too, had crammed a lifetime's worth of work into little more than a quarter century. Like Hutchins, Adler was a scholarship student. (He remembered standing next to the future Justice Douglas, a Columbia Law School student, waiting in line for a scholarship voucher at the bursar's office.) His father's jewelry business was not prospering after World War I, and Adler agreed to walk the twenty-five blocks down Broadway to save sixty cents a week, and to make his own lunch, to husband the two dollars a week in spending money his family could give him. Like Hutchins, Adler made himself noticed as an undergraduate. The same John Dewey who had lured James Angell to Chicago had since moved to Columbia, where he was perhaps America's leading public intellectual, founder of the "Chicago school" of pragmatic philosophy, educational reformer, and more. The 62-year-old Dewey, known as "the Jove of Morningside Heights," intimidated the stripling Adler not one whit. Here is part of a letter that Adler slipped under Dewey's door after a lecture, taking his professor to task for "completely avoid[ing] any suggestion of a duality of subject and object, or of experience-of-the-thing and the-thing-experienced":

> BUT from the standpoint of the absolute monism of naïve re-
> alism and immediate experience, as you presented it, there is
> the following dilemma: *Either* the immediately existent dia-
> gram of the staircase changes-in-existence from moment to
> moment, *or* immediate experience is solipsistic, for the evi-
> dence of two observers reporting different things to be imme-
> diately present to them at the same point and at the same time
> cannot be accepted by either one of the two.

Dewey instructed his teaching assistant to tell Mr. Adler to stop writing letters.

A couple of years later, at a Philosophy Department colloquium, Adler, now a graduate student, laid into an important
Dewey text, *Reconstruction in Philosophy*. Dewey, known for his soft
speech and mild temper, was sitting just two chairs away, building
up steam. When Adler quoted a Dewey passage, and commented,
"There is certainly nothing of the love of God in this utterance,"
the venerable philosopher lost his cool. "Nobody is going to tell
me how to love God," he fumed, stalking out of the room.

Like Harvard president Charles Eliot, John Dewey also casts
a long shadow across this book. Unbeknownst to both of them,
Dewey and Adler would spend their lifetimes in public combat.
At Chicago, Dewey had been put in charge of the university's elementary school, where he pioneered perhaps the most innovative
educational curriculum in America. For Dewey, "knowledge is in-
separably united with doing," Louis Menand wrote in *The Metaphysical Club*:

> One of Dewey's curricular obsessions, for instance, was cooking.
> . . . Dewey incorporated into the practical business of making
> lunch: arithmetic (weighing and measuring ingredients, with

instruments the children made themselves), chemistry and physics (observing the process of combustion), biology (diet and digestion), geography (exploring the natural environments of the plants and animals), and so on.

Dewey's pragmatic philosophy had little use for the "alleged discipline of epistemology" so dear to the ancient Greek philosophers whose works Adler would spend his life proselytizing. "Dewey thought that ideas and beliefs are the same as hands," Menand writes, "instruments for coping." Dewey's progressive educational theories rejected the notion of required curricula and "worthwhile" courses like the rubbish that Eliot had just cleared out of the Harvard catalog, such as Forensics, or hour-long recitations of useless, forgotten texts. Those were precisely the courses that Adler and Hutchins would later try to put *back* into the curriculum, with much attendant friction.

That would come in the future. But in 1924, two things seemed clear. First, Mortimer Adler was never going to get tenure in the Columbia Philosophy Department. Indeed, he quickly switched to psychology. Second, Mortimer Adler was an unholy pain in the neck.

"I was an objectionable student, in some respects perhaps repulsive," recalled Adler, who peppered his autobiographies with similar flashes of self-awareness, e.g. his curious revelation that he registered the cable address "Analerotic, Chicago" with Western Union so he could be reached by telegraph. Early in their relationship, Adler described himself to Hutchins as "[e]asily intoxicated; is married to a beautiful woman; has no children but you never can tell; is not good-looking but quite loveable; Jewish and German by ancestry but anti-semitic and Esperanto by nature . . . always philosophical, except in water."

Adler, who awaits his biographer, had indeed married a handsome woman, with whom he had two sons. A notorious philanderer, he divorced his first wife after thirty-three years of marriage and later remarried an attractive Britannica secretary more than thirty years his junior. They, too, had two sons. "Mortimer didn't have much luck with women," Joseph Epstein reported in a posthumous appreciation. Epstein quoted from an Adlerian love letter that contained the phrase "I love you with the passions attendant thereto." "Between his first and second marriages," Epstein writes, "Adler became engaged to a woman who, with her boyfriend, had been hatching a plot which called for insuring him into the stratosphere and then, with the aid of her boyfriend, shaking him down and possibly bumping him off. Adler's friends had her followed by a detective, and when the plot was revealed, he didn't at first want to believe it, then spent months of depression trying to get over it."

In Adler's note to Hutchins, the phrase *except in water* refers to a famous scrap of Adler-iana: He refused to take the swim test required for graduation from Columbia. A few years later, the university would award him a PhD in psychology, but no bachelor's degree.

Like Hutchins, Adler was a fervent believer in search of a belief. Abjuring his parents' Judaism, Adler called himself a pagan, by which he meant a sort of deist. His oldest son Mark reports that "Judaism obviously had little effect on him. There was no Jewish tradition in the family whatsoever. When he read the classics, he found that the theology of the Roman Catholic church was quite important, and he became heavily involved with Catholic beliefs." It is true that Adler developed an obsessive interest in the neo-Aristotelian Catholic theology of St. Thomas Aquinas, and during the 1930s he became a relatively prominent Thomist theologian. In Chicago, Adler first worshipped at the

Episcopal Church of the Redeemer, high churchman T. S. Eliot's spiritual home in the Windy City. He married two Episcopalians, and at the age of 81, during a five-week stay in the hospital recuperating from a viral infection, he converted to their faith. Soon he was attending, and even preaching at, the highbrow, high-church, high-net-worth St. Chrysostom's on Chicago's Gold Coast, north of the downtown Loop. Rhoda Pritzker remembers seeing him at the annual Bless the Animals service:

> I went every year with my Yorkie, Emily Bronte Pritzker. She was losing her sight, but it didn't help much, she was blind last 4 years. Anyway, everyone gathered outdoors, cops on horses, dogs, cat, rabbits, with owners, waiting. Finally the massive door opened and who should walk out very first, wearing long white robes, carrying the biggest crucifix ever designed, but Mort Adler.

Fifteen years later, two years before his death at age 99, Adler converted to Roman Catholicism.

Mortimer Adler was impossible, but he was not boring, and Robert Hutchins liked that. Over the years they perfected an intellectual Mutt 'n' Jeff act, with Hutchins playing the stern protective parent and Adler the bumptious and unruly child. In multiple-page, single-spaced, self-typed letter after letter over sixty years, some of them mailed from offices on the same campus, Adler preens, struts, and begs for Hutchins's approval. Yes, they socialized, but Adler, the author or coauthor of almost sixty books and a dervish of a typist, adored the written word. In a typical letter, "full of self-pity," Adler asks Hutchins: "To whom else can I go with my problems, when they are of this sort? This, Bob, is the burden of friends. To be your friend, I've got to be able to write you letters of this sort. . . . To be my friend, you've got to be able to receive them."

When I asked writer Sidney Hyman, who knew both men for most of their lives, if Adler had been in love with Hutchins, Hyman burst out laughing. "*Everybody* was in love with Robert Hutchins! My God! He walked into the room and you couldn't not be in love with him. Humorous, ironic, brave, beautiful, un-flappable, dismissive of cant—" Hyman ran out of adjectives. Hutchins "made homosexuals of us all" was his friend Scott Buchanan's memorable comment.

Here is a typical Hutchins bank shot, from his Chicago files. In 1948, with the Great Books frenzy in full swing, he received a letter from the St. Alphonsus Convent in New York City:

Dear Mr. Hutchins,

I'm interested in finding out some of the forces that reacted in Dr. Adler's life to develop the high type of moral philosophy he has?
    I would appreciate comment from you in regard to influence Dr. Adler and his writings have been exerted and to what extent in our present educational situation. [sic]

Thank you very kindly,
Sister M. Saint Agnes

Hutchins replied, with a blind copy to Adler, of course:

Dear Sister Agnes,

I am sorry, I can't explain Mr. Adler.

Sincerely yours,
Robert M. Hutchins

At that first meeting in New Haven, Adler and Hutchins talked, it seemed to both men, forever. During the first three hours, they discussed evidence. Hutchins was interested in the legal exceptions to the hearsay rule: for instance, the occasional allowance of deathbed proclamations as evidence, on the grounds that men and women rarely lie when facing their Maker. "Hutchins wondered, quite properly, whether modern psychology might not throw light on these accretions of the law," Adler later wrote in his 1977 autobiography, *Philosopher at Large*, "either by supporting or by challenging the assumptions of the judges who created these exceptions to the rule excluding hearsay."

As evening gathered, Maude Hutchins invaded her husband's office with her baby daughter in a perambulator, took the men home, and started pouring martinis. The subject of evidence was soon forgotten. Years later, Adler remembered a Proustian moment in his first encounter with the beautiful, "lithesome" Maude: "She exuded the pungent scent of the plasticene that she had been modeling. The whiff of this odor produced a state of embarrassed excitement in me, even to the point of my blushing." Adler explained to the couple that he was reminded of a bygone love affair with a sculptress. The odor took him back.

"The immediate consequences of that Friday in New Haven were many and various," Adler later wrote. "The ultimate consequences changed the whole course of my life." Hutchins offered Adler a Yale Law School professorship. Adler, while not particularly happy at Columbia, couldn't bear to leave New York. He continued to work on evidence, and even coauthored two books on the subject. Hutchins had other irons in the fire. Within the year, he had been offered and accepted the University of Chicago presidency, and he again reached out to Adler. At a fateful meeting in the Manhattan Yale Club, Adler recalled, "Bob confessed to me that, in his career so far, he had never given much thought to the subject of education. He found that somewhat embarrassing now that he was president of a major university."

Well, yes. Hutchins told Adler, and later wrote in a famous essay, "The Autobiography of an Uneducated Man," that he hadn't learned much of anything at Oberlin and Yale. His time in New Haven, he reported, was spent "wandering aimlessly around and cutting up frogs. I don't know why," he added:

> I can tell you nothing now about the inside of a frog. In addition to the laboratory we had lectures. All I remember about them is that the lecturer lectured with his eyes closed. He was the leading expert in the country on the paramecium. We all believed that he lectured with his eyes closed because he had to stay up all night watching the paramecia reproduce.

Hutchins claimed to have finished one of the country's finest law schools "with some knowledge of the Bible, of Shakespeare, of 'Faust,' of one dialogue of Plato, and of the opinions of many semi-literate and a few literate judges." When he taught in Lake Placid, he recounted, he couldn't believe how uninterested students and teachers were in learning. Then as now, they just wanted to score well on those darned college exams.

Well then, said Adler, who was teaching the John Erskine books at Columbia and at the People's Institute. Have I got a great idea for you.

THREE

THE GREAT BOOKS
IN THE GRAY CITY

T HE UNIVERSITY OF CHICAGO was unlike anything Robert
Hutchins had ever seen. This was not Oberlin College in
agrarian Ohio, thirty-five miles from the nearest city, where students and professors dreamed of a more perfect world. Likewise,
Hyde Park was a far cry from the gentilities and elm-shaded
walkways of New Haven, Connecticut. Chicago in 1929 was like
the Incredible Hulk, America's second-largest city, bursting out of
its carapace, swollen with immigrants, capital, hustlers, poets,
muckrakers, ideas, world-beating architecture, and enviable energy. Historian Mary Ann Dzuback writes that in Chicago,
"[p]olitical and economic power was divided unevenly" among a
corrupt Democratic political machine, "bootlegging gangsters
whose most notable representative was Al Capone," and the
wealthy industrialists of the downtown Loop: the Marshall Fields
of department-store fame, the meatpacking Swifts, the reaper-
rich McCormicks, and many others.

In his twenty-year-long tenure at Chicago, Hutchins would
bump up against the politicians who occasionally inveighed
against "left-wing" professors when it suited them. He never met

Capone, although he liked to point out that the two men shared a birthday. But he saw plenty of the downtown businessmen. In fact, it was Harold Swift, chairman of the university's board of trustees, who hired him.

There is the famous story of Swift telephoning Hutchins in his Yale Law School office at 7 A.M. Hutchins had mentioned during a preliminary interview with the U. of C. trustees that he liked to get cracking early. The very next day, upon returning to Chicago, Swift rang Hutchins's office to check. "Hutchins was mildly puzzled," his friend Milton Mayer wrote, "because Harold Swift was known as a man who, like John D. Rockefeller, thought twice before making a long-distance phone call to say what could just as easily be said on a penny postcard."

The University of Chicago differed from the Oberlins and Yales of the world in another important respect. It was less than forty years old. While architect Daniel Burnham had been building his famous, temporary "White City" along the shores of Lake Michigan for the 1893 Columbian Exposition World's Fair, John D. Rockefeller was breaking ground for his Gothic limestone "Gray City" less than a mile inland, on lands donated by Marshall Field. "The good Lord gave me the money, and how could I withhold it from Chicago?" Rockefeller later commented. "It's the best investment I ever made." The setting was promising; both Burnham and Rockefeller were building on land adjacent to parks landscaped by Frederick Law Olmsted.

In a few short decades Rockefeller and his first president, William Rainey Harper, created something astonishing out of nothing—nothing except money, that is. Harper trumped even Hutchins in the bright young man sweepstakes. He had finished college before his 15th birthday and had been awarded a Yale PhD in pedagogy and Hebrew Studies by age 18. With Rockefeller's money and his own furious determination, Rainey had created a modern research university *ex nihilo*. Only two American universities had copied the research-intensive German model, which favored powerful graduate faculties in the sciences and humanities over the college, or undergraduate, curriculum. Those were Johns Hopkins in Baltimore and Clark University in Worcester, Massachusetts. By almost any metric, Chicago had eclipsed them and most other universities by the first quarter of the twentieth century. It had a law school, a medical school, a divinity school, a business school, and graduate schools of social service and of education. Its Philosophy Department, selected by John Dewy, whom Harper had personally recruited from the University of Michigan, had achieved worldwide fame. The Physics Department had two Nobel Prize winners, poached from Clark and from Washington University. The dyspeptic Thorstein Veblen became a national celebrity by railing against conspicuous consumption and the leisure class from the safety of the U. of C.'s Economics Department. In a 1925 survey of twenty university graduate departments, Chicago placed first in eight disciplines, and four of its departments finished second, well ahead of any Ivy League or major state university. Ten years later, a similar investigation of thirty-five academic departments nationwide ranked Chicago second after Harvard. Hutchins liked to recruit professors to Hyde Park with his trademark bon mot: "It's not a very good university—it's only the best there is."

Undergraduate education was not Chicago's forte. For starters, the students lacked the sophistication, real or imagined, of the East Coast schools. Almost all of them hailed from the Midwest, and 70 percent came from Chicago. More than half of the students lived at home, not at the university. The notion of working while at college, which seemed exotic to the pampered Yale and Columbia men of the young century, was the norm on the Chicago campus.

Chicago's undergraduate men and women mainly attended large lecture courses, and did not follow common areas of study. Before Hutchins, historian John Boyer writes, Chicago had "a rather incoherent undergraduate curriculum, dominated by particularistic departmental interests and substantially staffed by graduate-student teaching assistants, [a setting that] offered little intellectual distinctiveness." Hutchins's friend and longtime university staffer Milton Mayer called the college curriculum "an accumulation of unrelated oddments, no sooner passed than past." There was serious talk among Chicago's senior scholars of doing away with the undergraduate college altogether.

That would not be happening on Robert Hutchins's and Mortimer Adler's watch.

When Hutchins became president of the University of Chicago in 1929, he invited Adler to join him. The offer was well timed. Adler wasn't wild about moving to Chicago, but Columbia wasn't wild about keeping him on. He had been shunted among the psychology, law, and philosophy faculties. Upon receiving the summons to Hyde Park, Adler batted out his seventy-seven-page psychology dissertation in twenty consecutive hours at the typewriter. It was about the psychological experience of listening to piano music. It was the last piece of traditional academic work he would ever do.

Hutchins thought he could parachute Adler into Chicago's Philosophy Department, but they didn't want him, especially when they learned he would be earning $1,000 a year more than they were. Adler had been making unflattering remarks about the Chicago philosophers at cocktail parties in New York ("slop and bilge . . . goddam Dewized bunk") and the word got around. Hutchins had to stash Adler in the law school instead.* In the same vein, Hutchins tried to appoint three of Adler's cronies to a specially formed Committee on the Liberal Arts, created to circumvent faculty scrutiny. But the Faculty Senate fought back, and clipped Hutchins's wings for good measure. Two of the cronies in question, Scott Buchanan and the improbably named Stringfellow Barr, known as "Winkie," stomped off to found St. John's College, the oldest and most prestigious all-Great-Books-all-the-time college in the world.

Even before Hutchins set foot on campus, the faculty was proposing to reform the undergraduate curriculum. Hutchins seized on the program, which immediately became known as the New Plan, or the Hutchins Plan. This divided the university into a two-year undergraduate college and four Upper Divisions: Biological Sciences, Physical Sciences, Social Sciences, Humanities. Especially promising high school students could enter the undergraduate college after tenth grade, if they passed an entrance exam. The New Plan inaugurated yearlong general courses on a pass-fail basis, with students not required to attend lectures or seminars. (Counterintuitively, freshman attendance rose 1.3 percent in the Plan's first year.) In lieu of written exams, the students had to pass comprehensive oral exams administered by professors outside the U. of C. system.

The tenured faculty could rule the Divisions; Hutchins concentrated his attention on the college. "The purpose of higher education," Hutchins thundered, "is to unsettle the minds of young

---

*Adler's abrasiveness cannot be understated. In an oral history interview, George Dell asked Adler about the rumor that he had hastened the death of Chicago philosopher and Dewey protégé George Herbert Mead, who resigned his chair while warring with Adler and Hutchins. Adler allowed that yes, he was quite abrasive, and that yes, he and Mead had disagreements. "But I mean, after all, that didn't kill him. [Laughter]"

men, to widen their horizons, to inflame their intellects." He loved Woodrow Wilson's line, that a university should produce young men "as unlike their fathers as possible."

But the 1930 reforms were only the beginning, in Hutchins's and Adler's view. The problem with undergraduate education was that kids didn't really learn anything. Whereas nineteenth-century colleges had once celebrated a liberal arts education—*liberal* here derived from the Latin adjective *libera*, or "free"; a liberal education was deemed to be one that freed students—now it just prepared students for the professions, or for nothing. To Hutchins and Adler, specialization meant vocational education, which was not education at all. Far from freeing students, it locked them up, treating them as objects of production. It was all very well for upper-class children to study English and History at Harvard and Yale; their ticket into the professions had been printed at birth. But the sons and daughters of Middle America, almost all of them the first generation in their family to attend college, had other goals. They were working their way through college, in many cases, to become the first member of their family to hold down a white-collar job.

For the first two years of college, Hutchins and Adler had far bolder ideas than those of the New Plan. Startlingly, they began talking up the medieval Trivium—grammar, rhetoric, and logic—and the Quadrivium—arithmetic, geometry, astronomy, and music—as the true basis of a secondary education.* Cribbing

---

* This could not have been as jarring as when Adler interrupted a discussion at a Physics Department lunch at the faculty club to hold forth on . . . angelology. The physicists were talking about Niels Bohr's observation that an electron can pass from one orbit to another without traversing space. Why, that's just like the angels! Adler explained to the roomful of men who had probably never been exposed to the Scholastics' vision of particle physics before. "Far from persuading the physicists that angelology might be a respectable science," Adler recalled, "my remarks on the subject, delivered with some heat and without any apology, generated doubts about my sanity as well as fears of a recrudescence of medievalism—the hobgoblin of a modern university dominated by experimental or empirical science."

from the educational ideology of the Middle Ages, Hutchins divided learning into four arts: natural, useful, liberal, and fine arts. Under useful arts he lumped medicine, navigation, engineering, and stenography(!). He called the liberal arts "contemplation and regular manipulation of things as symbols with an eye to the truth" and the fine arts "regular cooperations which clarify the truths of individual things in themselves, and thus render them symbols of other things." Facts are the enemy, Hutchins railed, in several highly publicized university speeches of the early 1930s. "Facts are the core of an anti-intellectual curriculum. . . . Facts do not solve problems. . . . The gadgeteers and data collectors, masquerading as scientists, have threatened to become the supreme chieftains of the scholarly world." The university's scientists and social scientists had no doubt who the "gadgeteers and data collectors" were. The enemy, according to Hutchins, was them.

When he published his educational *summa*, *The Higher Learning in America*, in 1936, Hutchins put all his cards on the table. The true subject of undergraduate education should be metaphysics, which, following Aristotle, he called "the highest science, the first science." "The aim of higher education is wisdom," Hutchins wrote. "Wisdom is knowledge of principles and causes. Metaphysics deals with the highest principles and causes. Therefore metaphysics is the highest wisdom."

How can students achieve wisdom? Not by sitting in a classroom listening to teachers lecture, and not from textbooks, either. Enter the Great Books, and the John Erskine pedagogy of Socratic, or shared, inquiry between teacher and pupil: "If he uses the great books as the material read and discussed," Hutchins wrote, "even the ordinary teacher (if he properly regards himself as a student of the great books along with his students) can perform the Socratic function and service—can ask questions which are genuinely questions in his own mind, because he is still himself a learner in the presence of the great books."

So the children of the Midwestern bourgeoisie were going to learn metaphysics, whether they wanted to or not. Hutchins, at heart a freethinker, hated what passed for freedom in undergraduate education. "The free elective system as Mr. Eliot introduced it at Harvard and as Progressive Education [read: Dewey] adapted it to lower age levels amounted to a denial that there was content to education," he sneered. From his perch atop Columbia University, Dewey declared that Hutchins's autocratic views on basic education smacked of fascism. This kindled a lifelong exchange of impolitic comments from the two men, with Dewey reserving special contempt for the Great Books educational formula: "The idea that an adequate education of any kind can be obtained by means of a miscellaneous assortment of 100 books, more or less, is laughable, when viewed practically."

Hutchins intended to prove his critics wrong. He would teach the classics to his undergraduates, and he would do it himself.

For the fall semester of 1930, Hutchins's first full year at Chicago, the following entry appeared in the catalog:

General Survey

General Honors Course 110—Readings in the classics of Western European literature. Limited to 20 by invitation. This is a two-year course, one two-hour class session each week. Credit is deferred until completion of the course.

The students knew that Hutchins himself would be teaching the class, and the limited enrollment added cachet to the unusual experiment. Eighty students applied for seats in what would quickly become one of the most famous undergraduate courses in the country. One of the first students was Katharine Meyer, who would become famous as Kay Graham, owner of the *Washington Post*. Meyer had transferred to the University of Chicago from Vassar because she had spotted Hutchins's "young, handsome, dynamic" picture in *Redbook*. As the students cowered around an oblong table, she recalled: "For the whole two hours, the two men hammered away, bullying us unmercifully—'Well, Miss Meyer, tell us in your own words what Aristotle thinks about this.' 'What do you think about what he says?' 'Do you really think that good behavior follows from good values?' 'What are good habits?' What are good values?'"

"The methods they used often taught you most about bullying *back*," she added: "about standing up to Hutchins and Adler, about challenging them and fundamentally pleasing them by doing it with gusto and verve, so that they were amused."

"What we gained was knowledge that we would never have gained ourselves," Graham's friend and contemporary Sydney Hyman remembers. "These are writers we never would have learned about in a million years: Quintilian's Rhetorical Exercises? St. Thomas Aquinas? I was raised an Orthodox Jew. It was a world we never would have known."

"Never were egos so quickly deflated," alumnus George McElroy reminisced for the university magazine:

> We had been supposed to start with *The Iliad* but Hutchins could not make it that week, so we had it and *The Odyssey* together. Adler had told us that he tended to go around the table calling on students, while Hutchins preferred to go down the class roll. The first name Hutchins noted was Dick Cragg.

"Mr. Cragg," said Hutchins, "there has been some discussion as to whether these two books were written by the same person. Do you find them alike or different?"

Dick's newly grown Adam's apple bobbed. "Well, they both have a lot of fighting—someone's always crashing someone over the head."

"Then," asked Hutchins, his right eyebrow cocking in what we came to know as his devilish-amusement warning (he had wrinkles slanting up over that eyebrow from its frequent use), "Mr. Cragg, when you pick up a book and find that, in this book, Soldier A 'crashes' Soldier B over the head, you exclaim, 'Ah, this is Homeric!'?"

"Hutchins liked to play such games," McElroy remembered, "often asking some unusually tricky question and then leaning back and blowing eloquently perfect smoke rings while a student floundered."

The critic Susan Sontag, who arrived in Hyde Park a few years after McElroy and Graham, came to Chicago for similar reasons, after reading an article about Hutchins's college in *Collier's* magazine. It was "about this eccentric place, which didn't have a football team, where all people did was study," she later recalled, "and where they talked about Plato and Aristotle and Aquinas day and night. I thought, that's for me."

Sontag married Philip Rieff, one of her teachers, and when he landed a job at Brandeis, she transferred to Harvard. "Harvard was a superb university," she said, "but still, an ordinary university, with a big menu, and no 'right way.'"

Keeping Hutchins amused was of paramount importance, and the Great Books classes achieved this. Hutchins loved controversy, and he loved the querulous reaction of mainstream aca-

Mortimer Adler and Milton Mayer teach the Great Books at "Mr. Hutchins's university."

demics to the news emerging from Chicago, that the undergraduates were "dialoguing" with the ancient greats. Nothing could have pleased the young president more than to confront a gray-bearded Chicago classicist on the neo-Ivy walkways of Mr. Rockefeller's university:

> "Mr. President, I understand that you and Mr. Adler are reading and discussing great books with the very young at the rate of one a week. I don't see how you can do that. When I was a senior at Harvard, it took us a whole year to study Dante's *Divine Comedy* under Professor Grandgent."
>
> Hutchins's reply came quick as lightning and was stunning because of its speed: "The difference, Professor Shorey, is that our students are bright."

Adler merchandises much the same anecdote, although his encounter takes place on the Midway Plaisance, the broad, Olmsted-landscaped garden mall that bisects the Chicago campus. He gleefully described to a friend how a pillar of the Chicago Philosophy Department bearded him one day after lunch:

> "You aren't having your students read Hegel's *Phenomenology*, are you?"
>
> To which I answered, "Sure, why not?" "Oh," he said, "I've never been able to understand it."
>
> And I replied, "Well, then, they certainly should fail to understand at least as well as you."

The Great Books seminar had its desired effect. Chicago was no longer Mr. Harper's or Mr. Rockefeller's university. It was Mr. Hutchins's university. Harold Swift said that he and the trustees took "a gamble on youth and brilliancy" by hiring Hutchins, and the gamble was paying off. Chicago craved attention, and it was getting attention. Even before the stock market crash that coincided almost exactly with Hutchins's arrival on campus, the trustees assumed that Hutchins would be a magnet for alumni giving and for foundations grants.

He was. The president's office was ground zero for big ideas. Hutchins tried to merge the U. of C. with Northwestern University, twenty-five miles away on the other side of the city. The notion that Chicago would swallow up all of Northwestern's graduate departments, and that Northwestern would take all of Chicago's undergrads, was dead on arrival. Later, a wealthy patron offered to endow an engineering school, and Hutchins turned him down flat. "Hutchins had a certain disdain of material things," historian William McNeill wrote, "and perhaps felt that engineering was a trade more than a profession."

The young president gained national fame, and regional infamy, for eliminating the university's storied football program, the Monsters of the Midway, once coached by the legendary Amos Alonzo Stagg, who enjoyed tenure at Chicago's Department of Physical Culture and Athletics. That took guts. "Football dominated undergraduate life every fall," McNeill wrote. "The worth of university, in their eyes, and in those of most of the citizens of Chicago, was measured mainly by athletic success." But the team that had produced the nation's first Heisman Trophy winner was losing money and losing games. In its final year, it lost 61–0 to Harvard, 85–0 to Michigan, and even to humble Beloit. Hutchins, a confirmed sybarite—"Whenever I feel like exercising, I lie down until that feeling goes away," he once said—unleashed his mordant wit on the football boosters, memorably declaring that "[f]ootball is to education as bullfighting is to agriculture." "There are two ways to have a great university," Hutchins thundered. "It must have either a great football team or a great president." On behalf of Chicago, he chose.

Chicago suddenly became the most talked-about university in America. In 1935, *Time* magazine splashed Hutchins's face on its cover and spared no horses hailing the "golden boy of U.S. education." Before television news, *Time* and its sister publication, *Life* magazine, *were* the news, along with radio and the daily newspaper. He shared its pages with the most pressing news, gossip, and diversions of the day. In the same issue with Hutchins on the cover, *Time* reported that the fledgling Nazi dictatorship was working on the economic subversion of the Polish city of Danzig, which it would annex four year later, on the second day of World

War II; that conductor Arturo Toscanni had just met Mickey Mouse; and "Eleanor Roosevelt Spends a Night in the White House," doubtless some arcane "in" joke.

In its cover story *Time* gushed, "A lucid, original mind, engaging presence and quiet, incisive delivery make Bob Hutchins one of the ablest and most popular public speakers in the land." The breathless prose went on and on: "Hutchins, once the youngest and handsomest big-university president in the land, is now only the handsomest. After six years of guiding a great university through Depression he stands not on his promise but on his performance."

Time-Life founder Henry Luce was a college classmate of the "prodigious Yaleman Hutchins," as *Time* called him. Luce's stable of magazines, *Time*, *Life*, and *Fortune*, would churn out generally uncritical agitprop on Hutchins and Adler and the Great Books for decades. In this outing, Hutchins reaped full credit for the innovative New Plan: "The Plan works," *Time* reported, while admitting that "there are no tangible tests of success for such a scheme." And more: "Applicants write in from all corners of the land, half of them saying they want to enter the University of Chicago solely because of the New Plan. Given a chance to proceed under their own steam, students have found that learning is exciting. They pile into extra lecture sessions just for the fun of it." The lengthy profile ended with a juicy tidbit: that Washington "was rife with rumors that [Hutchins] was slated for a front-rank New Deal job." These rumors, which were true, would persist throughout Roosevelt's years in office; Hutchins whispered for a seat on the Federal Communications Commission. Hutchins bruited for the Securities and Exchange Commission. In the end, Hutchins and Roosevelt could never close the deal. FDR needed a political commitment from

Glamour on the Midway: Robert and Maude Hutchins leave a university function.

the high-minded university president, but party politics was one game Hutchins just couldn't play.

In 1935, Hutchins was pure box office, and his beautiful, standoffish wife added to his mystique. "Maude Hutchins has been roundly criticized for snobbishness," *Time* wrote, but promptly excused her reserve: She was an artist "with a mind of her own . . . who ably sculpts and draws." Hutchins's biographer Harry Ashmore was less charitable, calling Maude "constitutionally disinterested in most of mankind." Two years after *Time* visited, Maude scandalized the university by sending out a Christmas card with a nude drawing of her young daughter Franja on the front. There is no recorded reaction from Hutchins, although this might have been the first public hint of trouble in paradise. Later in life, Hutchins explained why he never wrote an autobiography: "What could I say about my first marriage?"

Hutchins had a droll sense of humor that rarely failed to charm. In his very first speech to students, he proclaimed, "To become President of a University with a student body so numerous, so intelligent, and, may I add, so handsome would be gratifying to anyone in education." He teased Adler about overteaching St. Thomas Aquinas, "lest auld Aquinas be forgot." Hutchins spent plenty of time putting the arm on the Harold Swifts and the Marshall Fields of the world, all the while maintaining a healthy cynicism about fund-raising. He defined a "donor as a 'rich man who preferred professors to racehorses.'" In his desk drawer, Hutchins kept a sign that he pulled out only occasionally, presumably when Swift, the chairman of the board of trustees, was absent. The sign read, "We launder dirty money."

The future novelist Saul Bellow, who attended U. of C. for two years and later went to work for Adler, cottoned to Hutchins and "his incomparable WASP grandeur": "An Aristotelian and a Thomist, he saw to it that the huge fortunes amassed in slaughterhouses and steel mills were spent teaching generations of students the main achievements of Western culture."

When Bellow and his friend Isaac Rosenfeld arrived in New York as hot-to-succeed young intellectuals,

[f]or some reason neither Isaac nor I could think of ourselves as provincials in New York. Possibly the pride of R. M. Hutchins shielded us. For him the U. of C. didn't have to compete with the Ivy League, it was obviously superior. It never entered our minds that we had lost anything in being deprived of Eastern advantages. So we came armored in self-confidence, and came to conquer. Ridiculous boys.

Bellow was more cool-eyed on the subject of Adler:

I am grateful also to certain academics whose classrooms anticipated the Theater of the Absurd. Mortimer Adler had much to tell us about Aristotle's *Ethics*, but I had only to look at him, even as an undergraduate, to see that he had nothing useful to offer on the conduct of life. He lectured on Prudence, or Magnanimity. It was—well, tomfoolery.

Hutchins and Adler were putting on a show, and they were attracting quite an audience. In the 1930s, the nation passed through Chicago in a way it doesn't anymore. New Yorkers who were headed for the West Coast on the Century Limited or the Commodore Vanderbilt trains generally stopped in Chicago, often for several nights, before catching the City of Los Angeles or the City of San Francisco to California. Some celebrities headed for the ornate Pump Room at the Ambassador Hotel, ground zero for the newspaper gossip columnists, to be photographed for the wire service syndicates. But others headed for Hyde Park on the South Side, as General Honors 110 became a place to be seen. Hollywood bigs like Orson Welles, Ethel Barrymore, and Lillian Gish found their way to the Hyde Park seminar room. The best-remembered visitor was Gertrude Stein, at the apogee of her fame, who pounced on Adler and Hutchins at a dinner party at the president's house. The two men arrived at 9:30 P.M., because they had been teaching the seminar, which Stein hadn't bothered to attend.

When he walked into his own house, the first voice Hutchins heard was Stein's.

"Where have you been, Hutchins, and what have you been doing?"

Taken aback, Hutchins replied, "Miss Stein, Mr. Adler and I have been teaching the great books."

"Don't call me Miss Stein," his visitor answered. "Call me Gertrude Stein. What are the great books?"

One can imagine Hutchins reaching for the martini pitcher while Adler went downstairs and fished their reading list out of his suitcase. Stein perused the list and asked, "Do you read these books in their original language, or in English translations?"

Hutchins and Adler patiently explained that their underclassmen hadn't mastered many languages, so they taught the books in translation. Yes, they allowed, some style points were lost in translation, but they meant to expose their charges to the *ideas* contained in the books.

"Not so! Not so at all! Greek ideas must be studied in Greek, Latin ideas in Latin, French ideas in French, and so on."

Hutchins politely fumbled with a judicious answer, but Adler—who knew no foreign languages—went on the attack. "The argument grew heated," he recalled. "Gertrude rose from her chair, came around the table to where I was sitting, and tapping me on the head with a resounding thwack, said, 'I am not going to argue with you any further, young man. I can see you are the kind of young man who is accustomed to winning arguments.'"

At this point Hutchins's butler entered the dining room to announce, "The police are here."

"Have them wait!" Stein dismissed the servant with an imperious wave. It emerged that she had arranged a nighttime ridealong with the Chicago police department.

As the party broke up, Stein's companion Alice B. Toklas thanked her hosts profusely. "This has been a wonderful evening. Gertrude has said things tonight that it will take her ten years to understand."

Adler was buying none of it. "She was always saying things she did not understand," he observed, "as well as things she did not know had been said by others." Ever the gentlemen, he and Hutchins invited Stein to lead the following week's seminar on *The Odyssey*.

"We tried to persuade her to ask the students questions," he wrote. "[B]ut most of the time she harangued them with extempore remarks about epic poetry which she thought up on the spot, but which none of us, including Gertrude, could understand, then or in the years to come."*

---

* There are several versions of this encounter, and the above draws mainly from Adler's. Here is just a sample of Stein's own lengthy account in *Everybody's Autobiography*: "[Y]es I know and I began to get excited yes I know, naturally you are teachers and teaching is your occupation and naturally what you call ideas are easy to teach and so you are convinced that they are the only ideas" etc. etc.

FOUR

GREAT BOOKS
GOOD FOR YOU!

HUTCHINS MADE RUNNING one of the nation's great universities look easy. Of course it never was, most especially on
the money front. The Great Depression radically crimped everyone's style. Alumni giving and foundation grants fell off. Hutchins
took a cut in salary and scaled back the salaries of his administrative staff. For the faculty, he froze salaries, which actually increased the professors' standard of living in the deflationary
economy. However, economic austerity also doomed plans for
expansion and most ambitious reforms. Hutchins realized his
dream of creating a freestanding, classical college curriculum only
in 1942, with the appearance of the brief-lived "Hutchins College." Breaking with universities across America, the Chicago faculty voted to award the Bachelor of Arts degree after only two
years in the college. This controversial decision, quickly undone
after Hutchins left campus in 1951, partly validated Hutchins's
and Adler's insistence on creating a shared liberal arts curriculum
for all Chicago undergraduates. But just as important, the two-year
college addressed the exigencies of the war. Twenty-year-olds
weren't hanging around frat houses or leafing through Herodotus
in 1942. Most were volunteering for the war effort.

World War II granted Hutchins what he thought was his greatest wish: a little petri dish of an undergraduate college where men and women could receive the classical education he never had. World War II also rescued the university, as it did the rest of the country, from the Depression. Twenty-two million dollars— two-thirds of the university's total budget in 1944—came from government contracts. Yet the war also undid Hutchins, in a twist of fate worthy of his beloved Greek dramas. Casually, almost unknowingly, Hutchins made a decision that changed the course of history, and cast a pall over the rest of his life.

The Roosevelt administration had a secret project to harness the still-hypothetical power of the split atom for warfare, codenamed the Metallurgical Project. The important research was diffuse, being carried out at Columbia, the University of California at Berkeley, in DuPont and Westinghouse corporate laboratories, at a government lab in Tennessee, and at Arthur Holly Compton's physics lab in Chicago. Compton, a Nobel Prize winner and a renowned academic administrator, suggested centralizing the atomic research in Chicago. He had the clout, he had the excellent lab, and, in the pre–air travel era, he was the most conveniently located. Hutchins okayed the idea, although there is no reason to think that he had much of an idea what the "metallurgists" were up to.

The outcome was ironical indeed. Hutchins, who had been flirting with isolationism and pacifism before the December 1941 attack on Pearl Harbor, was suddenly playing host to Enrico Fermi, Leo Szilard, J. Robert Oppenheimer, and every A-list atomic scientist in the United States. And where did they build their "pile," the vast contraption in which they hoped to produce a nuclear chain reaction? Under a bleacher at the university's abandoned Amos Alonzo Stagg football stadium. Ever since Hutchins had canceled the football program, ample space was available.

The rest is history. Fermi's team succeeded in creating a sustained atomic chain reaction at Stagg Field, thanks in large part to Chicago's astonishing team of "data collectors" and "gadgeteers"— the brilliant research scientists whom Hutchins and Adler had been inveighing against for more than a decade. Most of the scientists quickly decamped for Los Alamos, New Mexico, where the Manhattan Project created the first atom bomb. (It was Chicago chemistry professor Samuel Allison who read out the countdown for Trinity, the first atomic explosion.) The aftershocks of the Chicago work haunted Hutchins for the rest of his life. He became an ardent ban-the-bomber after he left Chicago and always waxed apologetic about his role in the creation of the bomb. "I didn't really think they were going to be able to do it" was his too-revealing comment after the fact.

On campus, Hutchins continued to push the classics with ever-greater fervor. He once suggested forcing the U. of C. faculty to study the Great Books: "Outside of the Humanities Division, I doubt that three quarters of our faculty members have ever read a single great book." An instinctual cage-rattler, he once told a friend that if he had written an autobiography, he'd have called it "The Skunk at the Garden Party." Predictably, his quixotic espousal of bygone scholastic values engendered robust opposition. Some faculty members formed a "Stop Hutchins" committee, in opposition to the "baby president." His opponents spread rumors that Hutchins and Adler, who simply couldn't shut up about St. Thomas Aquinas, were plotting to convert the student body to

Catholicism. Historian Tim Lacy writes that the Chicago faculty thought Hutchins "was calling for the restoration of the medieval university."

It didn't help that Adler, wildly unpopular with the faculty, had a habit of saying and writing stupid things. In the campus newspaper, he published a lengthy essay called "God and the Professors," attacking the "anarchic individualism" of the reigning academic ideology. "I say we have more to fear from our professors than from Hitler," he wrote, idiotically, but not uncharacteristically. He also attracted the wrong kind of attention by coauthoring a faux-artsy, Dadaist nonsense book with Maude Hutchins, widely interpreted as a suck-up move and nothing more. Random House printed 750 copies of *Diagrammatics*, with line drawings by Mrs. Hutchins and prose like Adler's "Prayer": "Blue art thou, O Last, and deeply to raised; blue is thy pagination, and of thy fistula there is no wing." Mortimer, please.

But the Great Books idea stayed hot, even if not everyone was on board with the program. One group remained quite perplexed: the university's trustees. Board chairman Swift stood by Hutchins through thick and thin, but he wasn't overjoyed about all the commotion emanating from the Midway. It was bad for business—the fund-raising business, that is.

In 1943, a university officer had the bright idea: Let's take the Great Books downtown! Specifically, he suggested teaching an evening seminar at the University Club smack in the heart of the Loop, a congenial location for the city's movers and shakers. The idea had practical merit, and also spoke to Hutchins's desire to educate the world, not just students. "The best education for the best is the best education for all" was his dictum.

Hutchins sent out invitations to the trustees, their wives, and other titans of capital he hoped to soak for donations. The roster of the first downtown colloquium was quite impressive: Swift and his brother; Marshall Field, Jr.; Paul Harper, the son of William Rainey Harper; Meyer Kestnbaum, the president of clothier Hart, Schaffner and Marx; and Lynn Williams, the president of the Stewart Warner company. The class become known as the "Fat Men's Group," although not because the fat cats were overweight. U. of C. undergraduates had taken to calling the Great Books course "The Great Men's Fat Book Class," because some of the weekly readings were so long. So it was easy to rechristen the extra-mural version "The Fat Men's Great Books Class."*

Newspapers found the story irresistible: Business troglodytes interact with Sophocles and Saint Thomas, and love it! Piled on top of the national hype for General Honors 101, the idea began to spread: You can have your own Great Books group, just like the college boys and the Fat Men. "Perhaps word of the Great Books hasn't reached you," wrote *Chicago Tribune* columnist Marcia Winn in 1943.

> Chicago has embraced the Great Books so eagerly that book-stores can't keep a Great Book in stock long enough for the salesgirl to learn to pronounce the author's name. . . . [B]y fall our most adept gunmen will be tossing aside their sawed-off shotguns in favor of the Great Books, and their Studs Lonigan argot for the flowing prose of the King James Bible.

The university's extension school, which had been offering undersubscribed Great Books classes, was suddenly deluged with

---

* Milton Mayer, who sometimes stood in for Hutchins at the seminars, remembered Adler fretting about the ethnic makeup of their downtown teaching team. "[Morton,] a practical fellow, is worried about having too many Jews (beginning with Adler and Mayer) teaching fat Gentiles in an anti-Semitic club."

applicants. In 1943, there were 165 Great Books students in Illinois. By 1946, there were 5,000. Great Books programs spread radially from Chicago, springing up in Cleveland, Indianapolis, and Detroit. An editor for the *Ladies' Home Journal* declared that the movement was spreading faster than Alcoholics Anonymous.

Aside from launching a tidal wave of interest in the Great Books, the Fat Men's Group had at least one unexpected consequence. Two of its members, Container Corporation of America chairman Walter Paepcke and his wife Elizabeth, later founded the Aspen Institute, where Adler taught the Great Books to vacationing Fat Men and Women for almost forty years. ("I like to think he ruined the holidays of many a corporation executive by forcing him to read John Locke," Joseph Epstein wrote, in a waspish appreciation of Adler's life.) Paepcke savored the role of enlightened businessman and became famous in the 1960s for attaching "The Great Ideas of Man" to magazine advertisements for his box company, the Container Corporation of America.

Just three years after the Fat Men first cracked open Plato's *The Apology*, there were an estimated 3,000 Great Books groups up and running, primarily in the Midwest. "Everybody you meet belongs to a Great Books Discussion Group," reported A. J. Liebling, in an acidulous *New Yorker* dispatch from what he condescendingly called the "Second City": "The study of the Great Books can last a lifetime, even when the samplings taken of them are exceedingly small. (Two chapters of Gibbon, thoroughly digested in a discussion group led by one's chiropodist, are supposed to be the equivalent of the whole work merely read.)"

Hutchins's office became ground zero for the movement. Letters flooded in, asking for suggested reading lists, and for tips in setting up local discussion groups. Anybody who had a beef with any text published during the previous 2,500 years of the

A production of "Antigone," at the Aspen Institute. Mortimer Adler sits center stage, to the right.

Western tradition, it seemed, felt free to hold the University of Chicago president accountable. Sydney Morris from Highland Park, Illinois, complained to Hutchins that some of the books selected "so *shock civilized decency* that they are destroying the popularity of the course." Case in point, Francois Rabelais's *Gargantua*, in which he found these lines:

> *Shittard, Squirtard, Crackard Turdous*
> *Thy bung hath flung some dung on us.*

"*Gargantua* was never a great book," Morris continued. "It was condemned by the Sorbonne when it was first written and the vulgar of the world have dragged it down its dirty path to this day. Can't you see these lovely young mothers spending the afternoon looking up the meaning of dirty words they had never heard of before?"

There is no record of a reply from the president's office. However, the habitually diplomatic Hutchins did answer Mrs. C. E. Carroll of Libertyville, Illinois, who wrote in to complain about *Candide*:

Dear Mrs. Carroll,

. . . Voltaire was, perhaps, the single most influential figure of the eighteenth century, and Candide is his most characteristic work. I do not care for it, but I do not see how it can be overlooked.

With the Great Books catching hold, Hutchins and Adler decided to launch the Great Books Foundation, using some money from the university till and a grant from philanthropist Paul Mellon's Old Dominion Foundation, which had also bankrolled St. John's College. At the age of 33, Mellon, an unapologetic dilettante, spent six months struggling with the curriculum at St. John's after reading about the new school in *Life* magazine. Euclid stumped him. "Highly embarrassing for a Yale and Cambridge graduate," he reported in his autobiography, *Reflections in a Silver Spoon*. Undergraduate life suited him. "I bought a little house in Annapolis, going home on the weekends for some foxhunting, then returned by car early on Sunday evenings to catch up with my reading." He complained about his shortcomings in math to Carl Gustav Jung, who advised him not to worry, by return post. "Mathematics is not a function of intelligence or logic," Jung opined. "It is an asinine prejudice that mathematics has anything to do with the training of the mind. . . . I think you waste your time absolutely when you try to study mathematics."

Mellon, inspired by Jung and "longing for a more active life," left St. John's after six months and enlisted in the army, which seconded him to the Office of Strategic Services, the predecessor of the CIA. He would remain a lifelong supporter of the Great Books.

The Great Books Foundation hired outriders to spread the gospel outside the Midwest, and they generally met with success. "'Plato-for-the-Masses' Drive to Bring Classics to Public" was one of hundreds of inevitable headlines, this one from the *Christian Science Monitor*. Four years after the Foundation came into existence, there were 2,500 Great Books discussion groups all over the country, in public libraries, in church basements, chamber of commerce offices, corporate conference rooms at IBM and Grumman Aircraft, in private homes, on army bases, and, yes, in prisons.

The Foundation's newsletter, *The Gadfly*,* described some exchanges from the Great Books course inside Attica prison, led by Marius Risley and George Hertz. In the first instance, Risley is discussing the Book of Job, classic prison fare:

> RISLEY: "It seems to me that Job had some bad breaks in 'The Book of Job.' How would you react to a bad break, Mr. _____?"

---

* Socrates, in Plato's *The Apology*: "I am that gadfly which God has attached to the state, and all day long and in all places am always fastening upon you, arousing and persuading and reproaching you." The school newspaper of St. John's College is also called *The Gadfly*.

A forger, serving six to 20 years, said, 'You've just got to learn to live with the bad breaks and adapt yourself to them, because they're inevitable.'

"Are you a fatalist, then?" snapped Mr. Risley.

"I don't mean you have to go along with the whole stream, if that's what you mean," snapped the prisoner in reply.

Down the hall, *The Gadfly* reports, a different class was "verbally dissecting" *Hamlet*, which one inmate, serving five to ten years for criminal assault, found "sordid."

Discussion leader Hertz asked, "Did anyone feel any emotion about the killing of Polonius by Hamlet in the play?"

"No," replied a prisoner, "It's just like he was killing a rat." The prisoner, a former laborer, is serving 20 years to life for murder.

Even Hollywood got in on the act. With considerable fanfare, actress Julie Adams, the beautiful star of *The Creature from the Black Lagoon*, and her then husband Ray Danton, embarked on a suggested ten-year reading plan for the Great Books in the mid-1950s. "It's very hard to find anyone in Hollywood who digs Aristotle," she told the Associated Press. "I used to go around buttonholing people and saying things like, 'Do you know how great Thoreau is?' They would just cringe," she now remembers. "I probably bored them talking about it."

Adams, 81, still gets roles in *Lost* and *CSI: NY*, and still adores the Great Books, although she left the Beverly Hills discussion group many years ago. When I spoke with her in the spring of 2008, she and her current boyfriend were planning to tackle the new Richard Pevear and Larissa Volokhonsky transla-

"Black Lagoon"–era Great Books devotee
Julie Adams.
COURTESY JULIE ADAMS

tion of *War and Peace*. Adams still has both the low-cost Great
Books Foundation paperbacks and the stately Britannica volumes
in her Los Angeles home. "I wouldn't part with them, they were a
very big part of my life," she says. "Exploring life and what it all
means—those are the questions the Great Books ask. I wish they
were still everywhere. I wish the movement hadn't petered out."

Millionaires, murderers, gorgeous starlets, all of them cozying up
to Aristotle, and maybe even to Archimedes and Apollonius. In a
word: Why?

The Great Books craze gathered momentum at the end
of the 1940s, and remained relatively strong into the early 1960s.
The inherently suspicious Foundation figures claim there were

50,000 Americans enrolled in groups in 1947 and, after dipping to around 25,000 in the 1950s, rose back to around 47,000 in 1961, which coincided with the balls-out marketing push for Britannica's Great Books of the Western World set.

How to explain the popularity? Many reasons come to mind. Post–World War II America was creating a broad middle class, with purchasing power and a modicum of intellectual curiosity. The G.I. Bill for demobilized soldiers propelled tens of thousands of young Americans into higher education. Fifty thousand Americans graduated from college in 1920. By 1930, that figure had more than doubled. By 1950, the first beneficiaries of the postwar legislation were graduating, almost 450,000 of them.

Coincidentally, the notion of a "general education," or a prescribed program of study, was making a comeback. With much ado, a Harvard faculty committee deliberated for two years on "the objectives of a general education in a free society," to produce a 267-page report that undid Charles Eliot's curriculum-busting reforms of the previous century. Published in 1945, the Harvard study urged the creation of undergraduate requirements in the humanities, social sciences, and natural sciences "that would emphasize the heritage of Western civilization and endow all students with a common intellectual background," according to historian Timothy Cross. The Harvard graybeards basked in publicity for suggesting ideas that had been in place at Chicago and Columbia for many years. "Seldom has such an effort, two years in the process, been devoted to reinventing the wheel," remarked Stanford professor W. B. Carnochan.

In addition, the movement first dubbed "middlebrow" in 1933 became a flood tide washing across the land. In *The Making of Middlebrow Culture*, historian Joan Shelley Rubin offers a partial catalog of salubrious, intellectual diversions finding favor with

The first-year Great Books group of Elgin, Ill., sits for a portrait after its first meeting. Co-leaders Mr. and Mrs. W. L. Miller are nearest the camera.

The Great Books discussion group of Elgin, Illinois, 1954.
COPYRIGHT © 2008 BY THE GREAT BOOKS FOUNDATION

the middle class—the Book-of-the-Month Club, the popular histories of Will and Ariel Durant, newspaper book reviews, and the *Saturday Review of Literature* among them. Rubin devotes plenty of attention to John Erskine and to Adler and Hutchins. "With friends like these, literature needed no enemies," she concludes. The *Reader's Digest* launched its Condensed Books in 1950, just before the appearance of Britannica's Great Books.

There was middlebrow on the airwaves, too. In the middle of the twentieth century, it was still far from obvious that the broadcast media were destined to become an intellectual wasteland. From 1933 to 1955, NBC carried a show called *The University of Chicago Roundtable*, a weekly showcase for such luminaries as Hutchins, Adler, Enrico Fermi, Milton Friedman, Clare Booth Luce, and Saul Bellow. From 1938 until 1952, Great Bookie Clifton Fadiman—also a Book-of-the-Month Club judge—

hosted a popular radio show called *Information Please*, sharing the microphone with a member of the Algonquin Club's famous Round Table and with a *New York Times* columnist. In 1940, Stringfellow Barr designed a CBS show called *Invitation to Learning*, featuring Columbia's Mark Van Doren, the first man to coteach General Honors with John Erskine, and later, Fadiman. Barr was hoping to re-create a General Honors–like discussion on the air. CBS quickly fired the high-minded Barr, but the "longhair radio show," as *Time* called it, had a million listeners after three years and lasted into the early 1950s. Adler pushed his way into the early days of television, with a forgettable, fifty-two-part series of shows on the Great Ideas that ran in San Francisco in 1954. A publishing company that was hawking a pamphlet called "Have You Read 100 Great Books?" claimed that after the war, forces "have awakened—and reawakened—an ever mounting desire of countless folk to turn to books, not only for entertainment, but for education as well."

Southern College historian Benjamin McArthur offers another explanation for the Great Books brushfire: The god of scientific materialism, the animating ideology of communism and fascism, had failed. "Scientific materialism, the new coin of academia, was tainted by its association with totalitarian horrors and now seemed an inadequate base for democracy," he writes. "Hutchins had been preaching since the early 1930s that an 'education for democracy' must rest on the immutable tenets laid forth by the great works of our Western tradition. That message won a wide hearing in a nation hungry for guidance." Cultural historian James Sloan Allen seconds that view: "The world war was exactly the kind of cultural crisis—not just a political crisis—that Hutchins and Adler had predicted for a world dominated by value-free fact-finding, moral relativism and the distrust of intellect."

McArthur has another, simpler explanation for the attraction of the Great Books klatches: The groups offered companionship, "an attractive sense of community in the biweekly gatherings."

With an international war effort over, people welcomed a return to the neighborhood fires of their local libraries surrounded by familiar faces. "Your friends and neighbors will be there," a foundation promotional brochure promised. "You will meet your minister, banker, lawyer, company president, fellow worker, doctor, [and] grocery clerk."

In 1957, the University of Chicago's National Opinion Research Center surveyed 2,000 Great Books group participants, hoping to find out who they were. Then and now, there were almost twice as many women as men, and most not only had attended college but also described themselves as "educated": "They tend to be highly educated, quite married, somewhat female, disproportionately professional men and wives of white collar husbands; infrequently 'intellectuals'; under-mobile; possibly disproportionately irreligious; possibly under-proportionally Catholic; sociable; joining Republicans and Democrats."

The Great Books had come a long way from the longshoremen and soap-box declaimers of the People's Institute. "Factory workers and toilers were simply not participating," concludes historian Hugh Moorhead.

Not everyone jumped onboard the Great Books bandwagon. One speed bump on the road to universal culture was Miss Nell Unger, a contrarian librarian in Portland, Oregon, who was in no mood to drink Mr. Hutchins's Kool-Aid. In 1947, she rebuffed the overtures of the Great Books Foundation and accused it of being little more than a front for the University of Chicago's forthcoming commercial venture, the Great Books of the Western World. She cursed Hutchins for trying to shoehorn "the damned classics" into American education. "Ordinary people are not capable of understanding these books," Unger wrote to the Foundation.

More astonishingly, Dr. Jules Masserman, scientific director of Northwestern University's National Foundation for Psychiatric Research, lashed out at the Great Books in the journal *Diseases of the Nervous System*. "It is regrettable indeed that certain teachers of our youth revert to this form of medieval scholasticism at a time when old errors should be left to moulder in the dust of history," Masserman wrote. The Great Books were a form of escapism known as "substitute behavior," he insisted. "Other forms of evasion, he said, are "preoccupation with trivia of fashion, the spurious excitement of spectator sports, the false hopes of reckless gambling, the diversions of profligate sensuality, or the numbing haze of alcohol and drugs." Masserman scoffed that the books are selected by "intellectual betters and so attempt to solve all the unprecedented problems of today by the ancient artifices of Aristotle or the pert platitudes of Plato."

That pseudoscientific eyewash did not land on sympathetic ears in Chicago, where few men were strangers to the spurious excitement of spectator sports or the blandishments of the saloon. *Chicago Daily News* columnist Sydney Harris, himself a Great Books group discussion leader, answered Masserman in the vernacular: "Just stay away from Plato, doc, and keep your eye on Freud. That's job enough for one man."

The catcallers were swimming against the tide. In 1948, the same year of Dr. Masserman's outburst, Chicago mayor Martin Kennelly proclaimed the last week in September to be Great Books Week and erected a three-foot-high electric sign atop City Hall: "Register for Great Books." Not known as a bookworm, the mayor referenced Carl Sandburg, saying, "I think Chicago should be known as something besides the 'hog butcher of the world.'"

The city's cultural institutions played along gleefully. The Newberry Library displayed first editions of many of the works, and the Art Institute, the public library, the Chicago Historical Society, and the Natural History Museum followed suit. On the next-to-last day Adler delivered a lengthy speech on "The Great Books in Today's World" before an audience of 750 at the Fair Store, a famous discount store in the Loop. ("Everything for Everybody under one roof at a cheap price" was its motto.) He assailed his critics, including Masserman, and pulled out the rhetorical stops: "The Great Books movement aims in the direction of universalizing liberal education for adults—making it as normal as schooling—for children and youth, and extending it, as far as the franchise goes, to all students."

The week ended with Hutchins and Adler leading a Great Books seminar on Plato's Socratic dialogues *The Apology* and *Crito* on the stage of Orchestra Hall. For the Potemkin discussion group seated on the stage, they had drafted some very fat men, and a few women: the owner of the Hitching Post restaurant; the general manager of Illinois Bell; an appellate court judge; the city's corporation counsel; the president of the United Packing House Workers, a vice-president of the First National Bank of Chicago, and in some cases their wives. The opening question for the two-hour session: "Was Socrates guilty or not?" Twenty-five hundred Chicago glitterati filled the auditorium, and 1,500 would-be audience members were turned away at the door.

With the Great Books, it seemed, all things were possible. "I am not saying that reading and discussing the Great Books will save humanity from itself," Hutchins said, "but I don't know anything else that will." According to educational historian Amy

Apfel Kass, "Hutchins and Adler had transformed a technique of general education into a vision of salvation; they believed their Bildungsideal could save mankind and the modern world from moral decay and physical destruction. . . . The Great Books movement, in short, offered an intellectual surrogate for, or supplement to, attendance in church."

FIVE

THE MAKING
OF THE BOOKS

A MONG THE FAT MEN, one man was the fattest of the fat. He was William Benton, yet another Yale pal of Hutchins's, yet another minister's son, and yet another progenitor of the Great Books who simply couldn't think small.

By the mid-1930s, Benton had made a million dollars in advertising, always as an innovator, always as an idea man. He pioneered the use of cue cards (LAUGH!; APPLAUD!) to be held up in front of live audiences. When his company, Benton & Bowles, represented the Colgate Ribbon Dental Cream account, he dreamed up the notion that the cream not only cleaned your teeth but "freshened" your mouth. He was a mile-a-minute huckster who owned the Muzak Corp. for about a decade, hoping to create a demand for "subscription radio," anticipating the market for cable television by about forty years. He was a force of nature who later in life would prove to be a force for good. Back when one could do such a thing, he once ran out on a runway and hailed down a commercial jetliner about to take off, because he had missed the previous flight. Hutchins occasionally introduced Benton as a man who had a lot to apologize for.

Improbably, Benton, who hired and fired men before break-fast and became the first U.S. senator to stand up to Joe Mc-Carthy, lived in terror of his domineering mother, Elma. After he won a Rhodes scholarship coming out of Yale, Elma asked why a man would fritter away two years at Oxford when he had per-fectly good job offers sitting on the table in front of him. Benton turned down the Rhodes. When Benton left a promising career with National Cash Register to plunge into the uncertain, aborn-ing world of corporate advertising, Elma disapproved. "Dear Bil-lie," she wrote, "I am sorry to hear that you are going into a business that says, 'Palmolive soap is a good soap.'" Benson's biog-rapher, Sidney Hyman, wrote that Benton "grew into a man who seemed unafraid of anything, including God's final judgment—unafraid of anything, that is, but his mother's frown, while long-ing for her approving smile, which he never got."

In 1936, after reading in the newspaper that Benton was quitting the ad business, Hutchins lured him to Chicago. Benton agreed to work for the university for six months each year, as long as he didn't have to do PR work. Hutchins made him a university vice president, which disguised his true function: He was Hutchins's ambassador to the downtown plutocrats.

In the course of remaking the university, Hutchins had butted heads with some of the trustees. There had been a scandal involv-ing the niece of drugstore magnate Charles Walgreen, one of the city's megarich. She complained that she was being subjected to "Communist influences" at Mr. Hutchins's university. Inevitably her uncle started sounding off, and the right-wing *Chicago Tri-bune*, owned by Hutchins's blood enemy, the reactionary Colonel Robert McCormick, gleefully served as a megaphone. Hutchins dispatched Benton to Walgreen, and Benton smoothed things out.

Benton was an adman, and he understood businessmen without condescending to them. He was one of them. He settled Walgreen down, and even jawboned the crusty tycoon into underwriting the Charles R. Walgreen Foundation for the Study of American Institutions. Then Benton went to work on McCormick, and smoothed him out, too. Benton had charm. Benton had brains. And, like Hutchins, Benton was an idea man.

One day over lunch in the Loop, Benton was listening to yet more bellyaching from a U. of C. trustee, this time from General Robert Wood, chairman of the board of Sears, Roebuck & Co. In 1920, Sears had bought the *Encyclopedia Britannica*, but had never been able to do much with it. Sears's bread and butter was catalog sales, and its customers weren't sending away for high-end encyclopedias. The books had a market—surprisingly, half its customers had less than $25,000 in annual income—but they had to be sold door-to-door. Moreover, Sears didn't have the expertise to update the volumes, or the resources to commission new editions. In the past it had tried to enlist the U. of C., and then Harvard, into producing new versions, with Sears footing the bill. There was no interest. Most important, the *Britannica* was barely breaking even.

Inside Benton's head, lights were flashing. Why not donate Britannica to the University of Chicago? Benton suggested. After some back and forth, Wood agreed. Then it turned out the university didn't want Britannica. Too risky, the trustees deemed. So, in 1943, Benton bought the company himself and gifted one-third of the stock to the university, along with any profits the encyclopedias generated. Britannica acquired the imprimatur of a major research university, and Chicago got a no-lose gift, with some significant upside potential.

Now Benton owned a prestigious publisher. What to do with it? While he and his wife were participating in the Fat Men seminars, Benton had been complaining that some of the classics were hard to find in stores. Other people were having trouble finding them, too. The Great Books Foundation was losing money by publishing below-cost paperback reprints of some classic works that it refused to promote, fearing the taint of "commercialism." (As the Foundation encountered financial difficulties in its early years, Hutchins characteristically assured Foundation president Lynn Williams that "the ravens will provide.") The quality paperback revolution was still in the future. Books weren't cheap, and they mainly resided in libraries. Translations of the classics were in especially short supply. St. John's College had been forced to translate some of the Greats Books for its own, on-campus use. One Great Books discussion group had to drop *The Brothers Karamazov* because the Modern Library edition was out of print.

So Benton, who liked to boast that he generated at least 500 ideas a week, one or two of which might be worth something, had yet another brainstorm: Why not publish the Great Books? "What have we got a publishing house for?" he thundered. "Let's publish these books and make them available."

Hutchins wasn't keen on the idea. He said the university shouldn't be in the business of making "colorful furniture." Trust Benton—or Adler; both men later took credit—to come up with an idea. Benton agreed with Hutchins about the Great Books' fundamental unreadability: "The thought of reading them would terrify any potential buyers who would perhaps fail to buy if they thought they were supposed to read them." Suppose we published the Great Books along with an "idea index"? Benton suggested. This would provide a framework for Adler's contention that the masterpieces of Western thought "spoke" to each other in a Great Conversation, always capitalized to emphasize its inherent momentousness. So instead of taking the suggested ten years to read the books, you could look up *justice* in the idea index and see what Aristotle, John Locke, and even Fyodor Dostoyevsky had to say about the subject . . . without having to pull their tomes off the shelf!

Maybe the time savings would add up to two hours a day, who knows? Benton was a modernist apostle of efficiency, and if the index of ideas wasn't efficient, then nothing was. The game had been joined. In 1943, Chicago announced its plans to publish the Great Books of the Western World.

Adler would have been happy to choose the books by himself, and after everyone else had died, he claimed that he did. But Hutchins knew better how to navigate the academic kelp forest. A high-profile committee of great intellects needed to be convened, to commit great and visible acts of deliberation so that no one could later accuse the Chicago "medievalists" of packing the Great Books list with their personal favorites. Although, in the end, of course, that is exactly what they did.

Membership on the Great Books selection committee was almost foreordained. Adler and Hutchins, of course. John Erskine, who evinced little interest in the project, had to be a member. Mark Van Doren, who had taught the Erskine seminar with Adler and had become America's popular Poetry God, agreed to join. Two other bookmen whelped from the Erskine bloodline joined: Scott Buchanan and his close friend "Winkie" Barr, who were running St. John's down in Annapolis. Three other men rounded out the committee: Alexander Meiklejohn, progressive educator and a former president of Amherst College; the future University of Chicago dean Clarence Faust; and Chicago chemistry

The committee of once-alive white males, and their handiwork.
TIME & LIFE PICTURES / GETTY IMAGE

professor Joseph Schwab, the token scientist of the lot. Not every-one rallied to the flag. Librarian of Congress Archibald MacLeish declined, as did Lionel Trilling, Columbia's legendary literary critic. Trilling frowned on Great Books pedagogy in the academy, and thought the inevitable inclusion of difficult scientific texts doomed the Britannica venture from the get-go. "Such an excess of zeal or faith is likely to defeat the purpose of the enterprise," he wrote to Hutchins. Trilling, nothing if not practical, thought the editors' determination not to include commentary or explanatory footnotes further doomed the prospective Great Books reader.

Happily for us, the nine committeemen left a rich paper trail of their ten meetings that stretched over two years. At the first gathering in December 1943, Adler laid out the criteria for ex-actly what could be considered a Great Book. Each book chosen should

1. Be important in itself and without reference to any other;
   that is, it must be seminal and radical in its treatment of
   basic ideas or problems;

2. Obviously belong to the tradition in that it is intelligible by
   other great books, as well as increasing their intelligibility;

3. Have an immediate intelligibility for the ordinary reader
   even though this may be superficial;

4. Have many levels of intelligibility for diverse grades of
   readers or for a single reader rereading it many times; and

5. Be indefinitely rereadable. . . . It should not be the sort of
   book that can ever be finally mastered or finished by any
   reader.

The first meeting generated a "first string" list of indisputably
great authors whose works would be represented without debate:

Homer	The Bible
Aeschylus, Sophocles, Euripedes	Herodotus, Thucydides
Euclid	Plato, Aristotle
Galen	St. Augustine, St. Thomas
Dante, Machiavelli	Cervantes
Shakespeare	Galileo, Harvey, Newton
Hobbes	Descartes
Spinoza, Pascal	Locke, Hume, Rousseau
Gibbon	Dostoevski
Marx	Tolstoy
Freud	

Then, according to the minutes, the members set to bickering about the "second string":

ERSKINE: After all the discussions we had about the relation of the books on the list to each other, [and] their availability for comparison in the study of the humane tradition, I should have thought that Molière would be an inevitable choice. His best works are not only masterpieces of the theatre, but they are monuments of French thought, and they have provided a rich supply of germinating ideas.

BUCHANAN: I . . . protest dropping Molière.

MEIKLEJOHN: Wish we could keep him.

VAN DOREN: Molière will go out only over my bruised body. He is the perfect comedian, the classic comedian, and also he is universally delightful; he will be read by cooks and Congressmen with equal pleasure. . . . Keep him, in the name of sanity and sophia.

Molière would have to wait forty-eight years to be included in the Great Books relaunch of 1990.

In May 1944, the board took to voting authors on or off a list of potential greats:

[Marcus] Aurelius: 6 for; Schwab against.

SCHWAB: "He doesn't say anything. Highly teachable, but no real content. The fact that he was an emperor is the only thing that makes it good, and that is a bad criterion."

[Jean Jacques] Rousseau: 6 for; Schwab against.

SCHWAB: "Never so few fine statements set in so much crap. Not original or fundamental."

ERSKINE: "Not a philosopher, but one of the greatest spokesmen for humanity."

ADLER AND VAN DOREN: "Terribly original."

Melville: 6 for; Erskine against.

ERSKINE: "Of no such size, beauty, importance as Whitman; if Whitman out, then Melville out."

Dickens: 4 for; Erskine, Van Doren violently for.

ERSKINE, ADLER: "If Dickens goes, Melville goes."

SCHWAB: "Not really against, not really for. He's boring."

Mark Twain: 3 for; Faust, Schwab, Barr against.

"All against Twain want it understood they love him."

Duns Scotus: Schwab for; 6 for tabling.

ADLER: "Nobody knows about Duns Scotus."

Rousseau and Melville eventually made the cut, but Dickens, Whitman, and Twain did not. Adler was correct that nobody knows about Duns Scotus, the medieval theologian known as "Doctor Subtilis." There are several other works that draw a complete blank for the twenty-first-century reader. For instance, a lively debate ensued over the possible inclusion of the now-forgotten William Thackeray novel *Henry Esmond*. Hutchins told a colleague that "I asked Mr. Adler to read 'Henry Esmond,' because I was nervous about it. Mr. Adler asked Mr. Mayer to read it. Mr. Mayer asked Mr. Bellow [Saul Bellow, working on the Syntopicon] to read it."

Bellow said no.

Even more time and ink were shed over the possible inclusion of the Icelandic saga "Burnt Njal," the gruesome tale of Bergthorsknoll farmer Njal Thorgeirsson, whose enemies incinerate him and his family in their home. "'Burnt Njal' is exceedingly important," Barr told the committee. His colleague Buchanan "pointed out that it was the source of English common law," according to historian Hugh Moorhead, "and Van Doren made a case for its extraordinary contemporaneity, witness the Dumbarton Oaks conference," which in the fall of 1944 was trying to create the United Nations.

From the minutes, we learn that "Mr. Hutchins went on record as not liking sagas." He also blackballed the cornerstone of Norwegian literature, the "Niebelungenlied."

A year later, Barr was still tugging at the bone in a letter to Hutchins:

> *A month ago I reread Burnt Njal for one of the Washington seminars. Far from having overestimated it before, I think I underesti-*

mated it. It is not merely a magnificent narrative; it is not merely a penetrating study of human beings; but it poses the vast problem of how real law may emerge from a lawless community—the problem San Francisco [where the United Nations charter was being discussed] is now preparing to bungle.

"Burnt Njal" never made the Great Books list.

The committee members eventually dropped the Bible, for two reasons. First, they concluded that it was the one book Americans possessed, and they would own a version they liked. Second, Benton predicted that selling the Bible might trigger religious wars on the domestic front: "There are selling complications involved, where a Protestant is married to a Catholic, where buyers may want to exchange one Bible for another Bible after arrival of the set, etc. etc. Eliminating the Bible will simplify inventory, bookkeeping, and selling problems."

Benton rarely put his oar in, but others did. Milton Mayer, who often took the minutes at the committee meetings, threw in his two cents:

What about Hardy? What about him? He wrote the longest sentence in the English language.

Madre Dio, what about Pitt?

Wasn't there ever a Pole who could write at all? I am thinking of Szymczak, but Szymczak was President of the Northwest Trust & Savings Bank on Milwaukee Avenue.

When it comes to Great Books, no one is without an opinion.

Translations would prove to be a thorny problem, as one editor explained in a memo about the English-language Homer available:

Cayley, using a quasi-quantitative meter, which at first is hard to read, is a more skillful metrist than Herschel, but his diction, like Thomas['s], is somewhat precious and Alexandrian, in fact Spenserian; he also falls down on some of the "big lines." . . . Dart is often more felicitous in his phrasing than either Herschel or Cayley (he also uses a hexameter) but he is freer than either of the other, and often introduces his private theological comments into the text of the poem itself.

Pilfering from existing works would not pose a problem, as this same editor explained how to "borrow" a Gibbon text from existing publications: "It would be perfectly ethical to use the Everyman or Modern Library edition, if the bracketed notes by O(liphant) S(meaton) were omitted. If Gibbon's own notes were omitted as well, the length of the printed work would be cut down considerably."

The inclusion of scientific texts, like Ptolemy's *Almagest*, or Nicholas Copernicus's *Revolutions of Heavenly Spheres*, was bound to be controversial. Adler insisted on including them, but Adler knew next to nothing about science. The committee solicited the opinion of Harvard science historian George Sarton, whom they had originally hoped to include on the panel. They might have spared themselves the postage. "The classics of science are essentially different from the literary classics in that the latter are eternal, while the former are ephemeral," Sarton wrote, as if explaining the world to elementary school children. "Science is progressive, while art is not."

When Hutchins and Adler bridled at his response, he wrote them again, asking, "Don't you see the difference?"

> *"Hamlet" is something established forever, unique and irreplaceable, while each scientific book is but a stepping stone for the next one.*

Newton's achievement and personality are immortal; his book is dead except from the archaeological point of view. It is all right to study English in Shakespeare; it is all wrong to study astronomy in Newton.

Like Trilling, Erskine thought the inclusion of the science texts was ridiculous, but no one listened to him, either. Even Hutchins didn't hide his antipathy for the science books. "I must repel the suggestion that I have at any time said I would read Ptolemy, Copernicus, and Kepler," he informed the committee. "I would never think of such a thing (neither will any purchaser of the Great Books)." Hutchins, who often took a pile of classics on his frequent cross-country jaunts, rarely disguised his annoyance with many of the supposedly grand texts. Channeling the thoughts of a million undergraduates longing to leave the library and play Frisbee in the quad, he called David Hume "an ass." In a letter to Buchanan, Hutchins opined "that the Great Books seem either less great or greater when you read them again. I read the Modern Library edition of Molière the other day and cannot see how its inclusion can possibly be justified; it's trash, Professor, and nothing else."

Adler complained to Buchanan about Hutchins's "general ennui" vis-à-vis the selection process, and about his boss's "silly prejudices": "Worse than that, he is exercising prejudices about particular works, such as the Organon of Aristotle, the Laws of Plato, the Mediations of Descartes, On Christian Doctrine of St. Augustine—some of which I know he hasn't read."

In an interview many years later with historian Hugh Moorhead, Hutchins clarified what was not obvious at the time: *He* was the project's editor in chief. The committee worked for him, and he had absolute final say over what books went in or out. Hutchins claimed he exerted only a negative capability, vetoing, cutting, dumping the many recommendations, primarily because Benton had imposed a cap of sixty volumes for the set. Hutchins said that he insisted that only one book be included, *Tristram Shandy*, because it was amusing: "It's a very funny book, and I thought the set was a little deficient along those lines."

Having chosen the seventy-four writers, all deceased and primarily Caucasian males (St. Augustine's ethnicity is always in doubt), the bookmen now attacked the problem of the index. The concept was simple enough. They would hire a flock of recent college graduates, at $2.00 an hour, to read through the chosen 443 works looking for allusions to the 102 Great Ideas. Adler chose the 102 ideas, and never explained how he happened on that number, only that he was determined not to choose 100 Great Ideas.* These ranged from Angel to World, via Logic, Love, Rhetoric, Same and Other, One and Many, Time, Truth, and Tyranny. The random choice of topics was a subject of ridicule for years to come. When Adler sent Benton a draft of the very first essay, "Angel," Benton blurted out: "Where's Adultery?"

---

* Thirty years later, in one of Adler's innumerable appearances on William F. Buckley's *Firing Line* television show, a young Michael Kinsley asked the aging Great Bookie if he still clung to the notion that the Great Ideas numbered 102.
"Weren't you tempted by 100?" Kinsley asked.
Absolutely not, Adler replied, allowing that he might add one principle, equality: "The only idea that has demanded attention in the 20th century is equality."
KINSLEY: "Is that not in there?"
BUCKLEY: "How extraordinary."
ADLER: "I would add equality and drop nothing."
After Kinsley noted that even the Michelin guides sometimes downgrade their restaurant ratings, Adler allowed, "I might drop fate."
KINSLEY: "What's wrong with fate?"
ADLER: "It had its greatest meaning in the ancient world."
KINSLEY, bemused: "So fate is sinking and equality is rising."

Mortimer Adler surrounded by several dozen of the 102 Great Ideas.
TIME & LIFE PICTURES / GETTY IMAGE

Adler told him adultery would be indexed under Family, prompting Benton's reply: "What's it doing there?"

In a promotional film for the set, a world-weary Hutchins explains to Adler that "most of my friends are interested in money, fame, power, and sex—I don't see those in the 102 ideas. What are we going to do about those?" Flustered and impatient, Adler answers that the index has its own appendix, an 1,800-word "inventory of terms." Frowning, as if speaking to a thick undergraduate, he informs Hutchins that "your friends would be gratified, I'm sure, to find references in the Great Books to sex." Or would they? The inventory directs readers looking for the "good parts" to writings on sexuality by Aquinas, Hobbes, Darwin, and so on.

"War a great idea but not Peace?" media theorist Marshall McLuhan asked in a 1951 essay. When McLuhan saw a picture in *Life* magazine of each idea's file card stacked in a small box, he likened them to tiny headstones, "as though Professor Adler and his associates had come to bury and not to praise Plato and other great men."

Saul Bellow, who had returned to the South Side after finishing his studies at Northwestern, worked on the index. Newly married, Bellow was happy to have landed this "whopper of a job" that allowed him to read the classics on a bench in nearby Jackson Park, site of the 1893 World's Fair. Bellow described himself "as a sort of strawboss" to whom other indexers reported. "I, in turn, am responsible to Hutchins, and Hutchins to God and St. Thomas."

The real straw boss was Adler, who gave up all other university work to concentrate on the index. He fired off memos like lightning bolts:

> Aristotle and Aquinas are doing fine, but Kant, Descartes and Plotinus must catch up. . . . Under Topic 2B, I find only three references to Aristotle and three to Locke. This cannot be all. Something has got to be done about this. . . . We cannot rest on such a random collection with such a major topic. I am sure I am right. Don't give in.

In a letter, Adler recalled,

> *One man in charge of Aristotle and Aquinas would work 72 hours at a stretch, pile up $1000 overtime and knock off to go to the races. Adler would carefully record the fact that during the work on say, monarchy, nature and necessity, the worker had his mind on the ponies.*

Yes, he is referring to himself in the third person.

Adler and Benton had an amusing exchange about naming their index of ideas. Benton never thought *index* would do. Adler pointed out that both *encyclopedia* and *thesaurus* were invented words, so Benton set him the task of inventing a word for the index to the Great Books, a word that "gradually will become a familiar common word, no matter how strange it may seem at first." Adler vowed to come up with twenty or thirty possible neologisms, and he did, proposing *cyclopticon, topologue*, and *topolexicon*. Perhaps they might have become household words. *Syntopicon* never did.

Compiling the index nearly bankrupted the Great Books project even before it got started. Originally budgeted at $60,000 and intended to take two years, Adler and his indexing army of 120 staffers took over an entire floor of the university's Social Sciences building and burned through close to a million dollars— half the Great Books' entire budget—before Benton reined them in.

The Syntopicon emanated a distinct odor of flummery, although among the committee members, only Scott Buchanan set his objections down on paper. "Buchanan continued to view the Index as sheer folly and crude commercialism," Amy Apfel Kass wrote. It was "neither scholarly nor an interpretive aid," he complained to Hutchins. "It is simply Mortimer getting his staff to blow up to a monster his own bogus tricks of research, scissors and paste mixed with his today's current position in philosophy. . . . People will be disgusted and angry, if they ever look at it."

Even Benton, initially enthusiastic, started to worry about the vast size of the Syntopicon. In 1949, Benton sent Hutchins a letter quoting "a very revealing conversation" he and Adler had with his banker, Jack Janson. "Jack asked Mortimer how he would use the index when he wanted to give a speech about salesmanship." The obvious answer is that you couldn't. "Mortimer explained that there was nothing about salesmanship as such in the Great Books."

So Benton had yet another brainstorm: an "index to the index"! He called it the "Applied Course," a simplified meta-list of great ideas that would point out "suitable subjects for discussion at your Christmas dinner or at Thanksgiving. . . . After all, I want to read the Great Books in order to be popular and successful— and what are the applications that I would like to make of these Great Books that will help me and my child to become popular and successful?"

The Syntopicondex? Mercifully, the idea never got off the ground.

The Syntopicon eventually gobbled up 2,428 pages, the entire Volumes 2 and 3 of the fifty-four-volume set. The vast, unreadable index had swollen to 3,000 subtopics and 163,000 separate entries, not exactly a user-friendly compendium of 3,000 years of knowledge. In his Preface, Adler insisted the Syntopicon "is first of all a book to be read . . . [a book that] will take its place beside the dictionary and the encyclopedia in a triad of fundamental reference works." If he had a sense of humor, one might have assumed he was joking.

I suspect that Volume 1 of the set, Hutchins's eighty-two-page essay on "The Great Conversation," likewise went unread. More's the pity, as it is a beautiful, eloquent, at times humorous, and brief defense of the Western tradition told with Hutchins's trademark wit and conciseness. The slim introduction summarized the emotional arguments against modernism from "The Higher Learning in America," and also revealed Hutchins's state of mind in 1952—and where it was going.

"Great books have disappeared, or almost disappeared from American education," the Presbyterian minister's son declared. "We regard this disappearance as an aberration." Hutchins devoted a few pages to lacerating the progressive educational theories of John Dewey; the two men had been jousting in high-minded publications for at least fifteen years, although Hutchins's latest fusillade used humor, his ultimate weapon. He mocked (and of course, simplified) Dewey's notion that education should conform to young people's wants. "All young Americans of a certain age now want to be cowboys," Hutchins wrote. "I doubt whether it would be useful for the schools to concentrate on cowpunching in its moral, social, political, scientific and intellectual contexts." The purpose of education, Hutchins repeated for the hundredth time, is not to learn how to do something but "to develop a good mind."

"The products of American high schools are illiterate; and a degree from a famous college or university is no guarantee that the graduate is in any better case." This familiar Hutchins theme led to his call for a lifetime's worth of "interminable liberal education" as the *sine qua non* of "effective citizenship in a democracy." Toward the end of the beautiful essay, which prefigures the last few decades of Hutchins's life, he started to go off the rails. "We say that it is unpatriotic not to read these books," he wrote. "You may reply that you are patriotic enough without them." And now for the rhetorical climax: War is coming, he warned. Hutchins firmly believed that the atomic device developed on his campus would eventually, necessarily, be used by the United States or by the Soviet Union: "Therefore we must have world law, enforced by a world organization, which must be attained through world co-operation and community." Using the Great Books to "revive the great tradition of liberal human thought" can result in nothing less than "a world republic of law and justice." In other words, a Utopia.

When these words were published in 1952, Hutchins had just left the University of Chicago to spend a quarter century promoting the idea of world government, inveighing against the arms race, and agitating for liberal democracy and universal justice. It would prove to be a very disappointing twenty-five years indeed.

SIX

FASTER, PUSSYCAT! SELL! SELL!

O N APRIL 15, 1952, the university and Britannica finally launched the Great Books of the Western World at a gala dinner in the Jade Room of the Waldorf-Astoria Hotel. The books had been chosen, the dreaded Syntopicon had been put to bed, and a special $500 buckram-bound "Founders' Edition" of the Great Books stood on the dais. Although impossible to read—Britannica printed the books in double-columned, nine-point Fairfield type; for comparison, my footnotes are set in eight-point type—the books were quite pretty. Arrayed on a shelf, or in a semicircle, the spines irradiated the hues of a muted rainbow, imitating the colors assigned to disciplines on academic caps and gowns. The literature and poetry books were yellowish. Theology and philosophy were blue. Britannica chose green for the math and science books, and red for law, philosophy, and the social sciences.

Nine long years had passed since the project began, longer than the Trojan War, someone noted. Setting the dial to maximum hyperbole and self-congratulation, speaker after speaker approached the rostrum. Benton, now the junior senator from his home state of Connecticut,* called the project "the most significant publishing event since Dr. Johnson's dictionary." Although he still owned Britannica, Benton had left the University of Chicago, naturally, because his mother disapproved. "Hutchins is marching to a certain doom," she wrote him, "and you are being dragged along to it by him."

Hutchins was evangelical in his praise of his own handiwork:

> Here is our heritage. This is the West. This is its meaning for mankind. Here is the faith of the West, for here . . . is that dialogue by way of which Western man has believed that he can approach the truth. The deepest values of the West are implicated in this dialogue. It can be conducted only by free men. It is the essential reason for their freedom.

Turning to his friends, Clifton Fadiman orated, "You who have bought the Great Books are taking upon yourselves part of a magnificent burden, the burden of preserving as did the monks of ancient Christendom, through another darkening, if not Dark Age," and so on. Hailing the "truly epic struggle to publish the Great Books," Fadiman said that Benton "will be remembered less for his political career . . . than as the man whose courage and vision made possible what is symbolized by the evening."

Sic transit gloria mundi. Of course, Benton isn't remembered at all.

Conveniently, John Erskine, the man who started it all, had passed away the previous year. Although Hutchins and Adler

---

* In 1950, Benton faced Prescott Bush, the father of one future president and the grandfather of another, in a special Senate election. Bush, an investment banker who was also president of the American Golf Association, courted Connecticut's putative "Yale vote" by posing in campaign ads with the college's famous singing group, the Whiffenpoofs. Perhaps the Yale men had trouble finding the polls; Bush lost by just over a thousand votes.

occasionally mentioned the "onlie begetter" of the idea they had been championing for a quarter century, the three men had grown apart. Erskine thought including the science texts in the Britannica collection was absurd, and he held up the pedagogy at St. John's College, where students performed the experiments of Galen and Hippocrates, for special ridicule. In his 1948 memoir, *My Life as a Teacher*, Erskine wrote: "To ask boys and girls in college, or adult students off the campus, to waste time retracing the literary gropings of outdated science, is in my opinion ridiculous if not criminal."

In addition, he thought Hutchins and Adler had blown the value of the Great Books way out of proportion. I found an odd, undated speech in Erskine's Columbia papers, delivered in French on "Spiritual Life in America." In the speech, written at the height of the Great Books' commercial success, Erskine mocked Robert Hutchins's wildly unrealistic prediction that 15 million Americans would sign up for Great Books groups, and accused the University of Chicago president of "vulgarizing the most puissant works of human genius" in merchandising the classics:

> Juxtaposed with the "Great Books" we have the "Great Ideas"; several years and millions of dollars allowed a group of studious young people to come up with a number: exactly 102. For each one of them, they created an inventory of the important books that analyzed these ideas. They had curious, at times depressing, results; it seems that a lot more has been written about sin than about virtue. Don't smile at this naiveté; Americans love to express their conclusions in percentages.

In a 1946 memoir, Erskine noted that some people (read: Hutchins) tried to turn his Great Books course into "some specific philosophy, and others have tried to expand it into an educational method for teaching all subjects. With these aberrations I have no sympathy whatsoever." "I was concerned with no philosophy and no method for a total education," he concluded. "I hoped merely to teach how to read."

Now the Great Books had loftier claims.

Even before the Waldorf dinner, Adler had been hawking the books like a benighted drummer from a Sinclair Lewis novel. Benton made him do it. With the Syntopicon madness threatening to break the bank, Benton had threatened to pull the plug on GBWW, and stop throwing good money after bad. Adler came up with an idea to raise cash. He pitched Benton on the $500 "Founders' Edition" described above and bet he could sell 500 of them to all the famous people he, Benton, and Hutchins knew. Could the nonswimming, "analerotic" Platophile sell? Benton was willing to give him a try.

First, Adler drafted a pitch letter for the money men, and sent it to Benton for vetting. The perpendicular pronoun gave pause:

> Mortimer, on your third paragraph I hope you won't object if I suggest that you reread it and consider carefully the pronoun "I." It is not "I, Mortimer Adler," who is trying to sell the Great Books or the patrons' edition. It is "we, the Encyclopedia Britannica." It is the Encyclopedia Britannica who has the big stake here and the big risk here, and if this were not true, I would not be sitting here at 11 o'clock at night reading your letter and pondering it and answering it.

The solicitation, ultimately signed by Adler and Hutchins, summoned forth 250 subscriptions. But Adler had promised 500.

So he spent six months traveling, cajoling and jawboning and selling. He was good at it. Paul Mellon sprang for 10 sets, to be distributed to colleges and libraries. Kay Graham's father, *Washington Post* owner Adolph Meyer, had always been a big Adler fan. He bought 15.

Late on a Friday afternoon, Adler secured an appointment with the taciturn Earl Puckett, chairman of Allied Stores, then the largest department-store chain in America. Here's my idea, Adler said. Buy a set of the Great Books for each one of your eighty-five stores, and have them donate the books to the local public library for some free publicity. Puckett didn't answer, but buzzed his secretary for a list of his store locations. Without speaking, he placed check marks next to roughly half the store names, and then rose to leave for the weekend. "We'll take forty-five sets," Puckett said.

Hutchins and Adler tried this same gambit with Conrad Hilton. They cornered him in a drawing room of the Twentieth Century Limited transcontinental train and proposed that he buy a set of Great Books for the lobby of each of his hotels. No sale.

Clare Booth Luce, Henry Luce's wife and also a big fan of the Western canon, secured Adler an appointment with Texas oilman H. L. Hunt, said to be the eighth-richest man in America. The right-wing Hunt was obsessed with the spread of "liberalism" in America and had been bankrolling various educational enterprises—"ill-conceived efforts at propaganda," Adler later called them. Adler met him twice, but couldn't close the sale.

Two days later, he bumped into Sears Roebuck chairman General Robert Wood in Chicago.

"Were you in Texas recently?" Wood asked.

Yes, Adler replied. Wood had just received a phone call from Hunt, inquiring whether Adler was a member of the Communist

Party. *The Communist Manifesto* was one of the Great Books, and Hunt wasn't buying.

By 1952, McCarthyism was in full swing, and even though the selection committee had purged left-leaning troublemakers like Thorstein Veblen and Vladimir Lenin, the *Manifesto* ruffled some feathers. When the Bookies showed up at the White House to present President Truman with his set, a Hearst reporter queried Benton about his promotional necktie, which bore the names of all seventy-four Great Books authors.

"What's on that tie? Marx?"

"That's for Hart Schaffner and Marx," Benton replied, breezily departing the press area.

Publication means reviews. Regrettably, Henry Luce didn't own every newspaper and magazine in America. Adler would later claim that everyone loved the GBWW, but that was not the case at all. Even his friend Gilbert Highet, who had taught at both St. John's and Columbia, expressed plenty of reservations in the *New York Times*. Highet called the set's omissions "astonishing":

> For 1,500 years the world read Cicero (omitted) rather than Aristotle and Plato; for 2,000 years it read Horace and Sallust (omitted) rather than Ptolemy and Archimedes. The education of the West has long cultivated Racine and Moliere and Ariosto and Tasso; they are omitted. It has seldom included Fourier and Faraday; they are printed at length.

Nobody understood why the scientific works had been included. In the *Atlantic*, another Adler pal and Columbia stalwart, Jacques Barzun, asked, "Of the score of scientists and mathematicians in the collection, how many are in any sense readable?" Even *Science* magazine, the official organ of the American Association for the Advancement of Science, noted that "few thinking persons are likely to linger very long over, say, tables giving for the 1840s, monthly magnetic declinations at Toronto, St. Petersburg, Washington, Lake Athabasca and Fort Simpson," included in the GBWW text of Michael Faraday's *Experimental Researches in Electricity*.

Writing in the *Saturday Review*, Harvard science historian Bernard Cohen echoed his colleague George Sarton's earlier indictment of the scientific material. "The 'great books' of science in this collection have only a kind of archaeological value" was the opening line of his withering review. Cohen pointed out that even men of science found works like Ptolemy's *Almagest* impenetrable, and read them only with the aid of commentaries. "While we must applaud the first printing in English of translations of Ptolemy, Copernicus, and Kepler, we must also ask what general reader will ever read them?"

John Leonard was among the many critics who unloaded on the Syntopicon's 102 Great Ideas, in the *National Review*: "We are never told just how the pincer-like movement of the minds of Adler and Hutchins arrived at that curiously frightening number. It reminds me of the radio advertisements for a beer brewed in Southern California, which went through exactly as many trial runs before being perfected."

The most hostile review of all appeared in the *New Yorker*, from the pen of Dwight MacDonald. This essay, "The Book-of-the-Millennium Club," is still used in writing classes, as a 4,700-word definition of *invective*. MacDonald mocked the selections, especially the scientific works. ("Infinitely unreadable.") He mocked the complete absence of explanatory notes, victims of the

Hutchins-Adler conceit that the texts spoke for themselves. ("Lacking such help, how can one be expected to take an interest in such problems, vivid enough to Aquinas, as . . . 'Whether We Should Distinguish Irascible and Concupiscible Parts in the Superior Appetite?'") He accused the editors of skimping on translations. ("Charles Eliot Norton's prose Dante is unbelievably graceless.") He mocked Hutchins's much-quoted, high-flown rhetoric at the Waldorf launch party. ("Madison Avenue cant . . . poppycock.") He thought Adler's philosophical work was a joke. ("A jungle of jargon, a Luna Park of 'nuclear agreements,' 'taxonomic questions,' 'explicative issues,' etc.") He couldn't stand the Syntopicon. ("One has the feeling of being caught in a Rube Goldberg contraption.")

MacDonald dared to ask, "Why a set at all?" And naturally he provided an answer. The GBWW aimed "to fix the canon of the Sacred Texts by printing them in a special edition. . . . In its massiveness, its technological elaboration, its fetish of The Great, and its attempt to treat systematically and with scientific precision materials for which the method is inappropriate, Dr. Adler's set of books is a typical expression of the religion of culture that appeals to the American academic mentality."

Well, everyone gets a bad review now and then. But a more important problem quickly raised its head. Just as Benton and his cohorts had feared in their darkest moments, no one wanted to buy the Great Books.

In 1952, Britannica sold 1,863 sets of the GBWW, which listed for $250.00. In 1953, it sold 138 sets. The problem was that the Britannica salesmen, who worked door-to-door, didn't much care for the Great Books. It was a lot easier, and more profitable, to sell a family on the world's greatest encyclopedia than to sell a collection of musty writings that for some reason included faraway magnetic declinations, whatever those were. Something had to be done.

After two years of anemic sales, Benton finally hired a supersalesman to fix the problem, one Kenneth Harden, who had been selling encyclopedias for thirty-seven years. Harden was a foot-in-the-door man, and he and Benton tossed the initial GBWW sales playbook to the winds. Let's stop marketing to the 2 percent of the country who are "eggheads," Harden argued. "Let's go after the mass market—the butcher, the baker, the candlestick maker."

Harden set up a special training program for his new, dedicated, Los Angeles–based sales force, "at which new salesmen learned how to use the Syntopticon [*sic*] and to pronounce the names of the authors. (Reading them is not required)," *Time* magazine reported. Depending on the quality of the paper and the luxury of the bindings, the books were available in a variety of prices ranging up to $1,175, and of course salespeople pressed their installment plan—$10 down and $10 a month, sometimes offering to throw in a Bible, bookcase, or dictionary if it helped to close the sale.

Benton wanted to sell directly into people's core anxieties, as he explained the set's "snob appeal":

> Good promotion and good selling interpret [the set's intellectual] promises in terms of the individual's basic desires. How does he become more attractive to the opposite sex? How does he impress people at a party? How does he learn what he needs to know in order to get promoted? How does he acquire the sheen and the glamor of people such as Hutchins, Adler, the Fat Man's Class in Chicago and the five hundred Founders? How does he impress the boss?

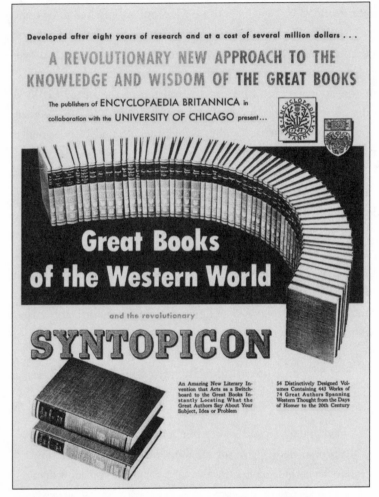

Light reading for "the butcher, the baker, the candlestick maker."

Simultaneously, Britannica carpet-bombed magazines and newspapers with its national ad campaigns. This text ran all over the country:

A problem? Consult this evening with the greatest minds of the Western world, grasp their precious wisdom. Start reading immediately at the point of your own maximum interest.

The ability to Discuss and Clarify Basic Ideas is vital to success. Doors open to the man who possesses this talent.

Thousands now turning to Great Books as increased life expectancy provides more time for mental recreation.

A Prime Source of Self-Improvement and an inexhaustible fund of adult entertainment.

The Great Books are capable of being both these things because the best entertainment is that which elevates as it entertains. When the current best-sellers are forgotten, the Great Books will still be great.

Ad copy from Chicago's Leo Burnett agency depicted a cemetery headstone, which read: "Here Lies the Mind of JOHN DOE Who at Age 30 Stopped Thinking." The ad continued: "Great Books alone can't make you a vice-president. Or Chairman of the Board. But they can stimulate your mind, and sharpen your judgment." The ads emphasized the Great Books' improbable "Ten Year Reading Plan"—competing with the Harvard Classics'

"Fifteen Minutes a Day" program—which theoretically escorted the customer though the fifty-two volumes (not counting the two-volume Syntopicon) in just under 4,000 days.

Britannica printed up endorsements from the celebrities of the day, such as Arthur Schlesinger, Jr., and Adlai Stevenson, who was a paid consultant to Benton. Stevenson "praised the product as unrestrainedly as so many debutantes endorsing the virtues of Pond's facial cream," Dwight MacDonald wrote, taking a second whack at the Great Books, again in the *New Yorker*. MacDonald proved to be the scorpion that couldn't stop stinging. He *hated* the Great Books. He trashed them again in a famous 1960 *Partisan Review* essay, "Masscult and Midcult": "It is one thing to bring High Culture to a wider audience without change; and another to 'popularize' it by sales talk in the manner of Clifton Fadiman or Mortimer J. Adler."

Benton didn't sign up just eggheads to hype the set. Boxer Gene Tunney extolled the virtues of the books in one national campaign: "Anyone can read these books with profit and enjoyment. And, because of your new development, the Syntopicon, one can sit down to this mental feast and select the morsels that are most appealing to the individual or to his interest or mood of the day."

The hype brought results. Just a few years after Harden's crew took over, Britannica sold 35,000 sets a year. In 1961, it sold over 50,000 sets, worth $22 million. The Harvard Classics were feeling the heat. Hilariously, Harvard started marketing "The Idexicon," billed as "a revolutionary new guide to the priceless wisdom of 300 years of civilized man. It arranges the great wealth of masterpieces contained in The Harvard Classics into major idea groups so that you can be guided in your reading. . . . With the

Idexicon you can 'tune in' to the thinking of great minds in every area of modern living. . . . It is as easy to use as a dictionary.'"

But the hype brought trouble, too. The Federal Trade Commission busted Britannica not once, but twice, for deceptive sales practices. The salesmen used a variety of tricks—among them, trying to pass themselves off as assistant professors from the University of Chicago. In a memo to his division managers in 1961, *after* the first settlement of FTC charges, Harden wrote: "We ran across a case today in Spokane where the salesman claimed to be a PhD from the University on a $25,000 a year salary. . . . Needless to say, we terminated his association and put him on the Do Not Employ List."

In one version of the masquerade, the salesmen would claim to be contacting potential scholarship students on behalf of the university. Russell Everett of East Paterson, N.J., wrote to Hutchins's successor, U. of C. Chancellor Lawrence Kimpton, asking if the salesman who had called him was really with the university's Research Division. And had Mr. Everett's daughter really been selected as one of thirty-three New Jersey high school students to participate in a U. of C. survey?

---

* Adler the irrepressible salesman firmly believed that *his* Great Books were far greater than any ever produced at Harvard. Just before the GBWW launch, he composed a five-page, single-spaced memo for Britannica management, highlighting the many superiorities of the Chicago set:

> *Harvard Classics: 22,462 pages, with 360 words on a page (average)*
> *Great Books: 32,000 pages, with 816 words on a page (average) . . .*
> *. . . the Harvard Classics . . . have the deadly appearance of a set of books. . . .*
> *The paper of the Harvard Classics is of a quality inferior to the paper chosen for Great Books. . . .*

Adler likewise criticized Harvard's use of excerpts rather than full texts, and mocked President Charles Eliot's vaunted fifteen-minutes-a-day reading plan.

On behalf of Kimpton, Secretary W. V. Morgenstern replied:

Your surmise about Mr. Corris being an encyclopedia salesman is probably correct. Salesmen for "The Great Books of the Western World" recently called a number of parents in Ridgeway, New Jersey, representing the University of Chicago and said it was interested in assisting their children in learning about college study methods. We . . . have been engaged in some vigorous discussion with the publisher about this misrepresentation. The University is not engaged in any survey, and it would certainly not undertake any inquiries to parents without full knowledge of the school authorities.

The ever-inventive salesmen sometimes passed themselves off as canvassers for the Advertising Research Analyst group, and asked the families they visited to fill out a questionnaire. "What would you do after you complete the questionnaire?" an FTC investigator asked one salesman.

A. I would read the bottom line of the last page which says in appreciation for the help you have given us I have been instructed to fill you in briefly on the Syntopicon and The Great Books Program and to obtain a few additional reactions.

Q. And then what would you do?

A. Then you started into the [sales] presentation.

The prepared script read like this:

> Hello, Mr. Jones. I'm Bill Smith from the Great Ideas Program. Someone in your family requested a free booklet, and I stopped by to deliver it. Incidentally, it's free.
>
> You're welcome, Mr. Jones. You see, one of the reasons we are delivering the booklet in person is that the company is making a study of the effectiveness of national advertising in each local area. . . . May I step in and complete my report so I can return it at once to our director of national advertising?

Another trick was to issue a "certificate" for a free vacation, or, as a complainer told the Commission, "Someone called up and said that our name was entered into a contest, and we hadn't won first prize, but we had won a consolation prize." The prize had to be delivered in person, of course. Sometimes they sold a fake research service, which amounted to someone Xeroxing a page from an encyclopedia and sending it to the customer. The Britannica reps also perfected a technique called the "Mexican build-up"(!), in which they would show a long list of goodies, assign inflated prices to each item, and then "discount" offers to levels above the actual retail prices. With the Great Books, they would present a "founders" price of $500 or $700, and then promise a deal at $350, still north of the then-actual $300 retail price. Perhaps this was a common retail practice in Mexico. Who knows?

The penalty for these shenanigans was stiff. After the FTC's Final Order of 1976, all salesmen had to hand their prospective customers a three-by-five-inch file card, with the representative's name, affiliation, job title, and the words "The purpose of this representative's call is to solicit the sale of [The Great Books of the Western World]"—in ten-point type. Each sales contract had to include a price list, stating in twelve-point, boldface type that "THE FOLLOWING PRICES ARE THE *only* AUTHORIZED PRICES AT WHICH THE LISTED ITEMS MAY BE OFFERED." "It was embarrassing and it sometimes made it harder to sell," says Charles Van Doren, the son of Adler's friend Mark Van Doren, who worked at Britannica at the time. "It was like the disclosure on a package of cigarettes."

In his memoir, *An Open Book*, critic Michael Dirda recalls "the young salesman, in short-sleeved white shirt and dark tie" who showed up at his parents' home in Ohio. The man cleverly

> neglected to mention the outmoded translations, the ugly double columns of type, the lack of explanatory notes and the 102 arid essays (by Mort) in *The Syntopicon*, that wrong-headed index to the so-called "Great Ideas" (among them Love, God, and Truth). Instead he offered the kind of snake-oil enticements common to all door-to-door fast talkers: easy monthly payments, a handsome bookcase thrown in, a free dictionary. I admired his patter and remembered it, a few years later, when I took a job selling Fuller Brush products.

Harden's dark arts started to lose their potency in the late 1960s. Not only were unit sales slowing down, but sales leads—the mother's milk of future business—were increasingly harder to come by. He and Benton did what retailing pros naturally do. They commissioned a market research study.

Carried out by Marplan-Chicago, the "GB Awareness Study" had some good news. The customer satisfaction rate was very high—90 percent. Only one-third of the owners said they used the Syntopicon, which surprised no one. Of course, owners "complain of too little time to make use of the GB," Marplan reported, "although they proclaim their intention to read them more."

The majority of users hailed from the engineering, technical, and service professions, and were interested in "present[ing] themselves well to others in terms of external appearance and behavior." So Benton was right. They were nerds hoping to get a date by yammering about Tolstoy or Laurence Sterne. Except these nerds were *really* nerdy: "The GB owners and prospects are 'loners' or individuals who find the greatest satisfaction in solitary pursuits such as reading. . . . The GB owners and prospects are *not* people-oriented and show little comprehension of the motivations of others. In fact, they consider people quite disruptive to their lives."

Here was the not-so-good news. Marplan identified a group of nonowners whom they called the "really awares." These men and women knew a great deal about the GBWW and the Syntopicon, plus they weren't socially maladjusted. Marplan said they were "more self-directed, socially oriented, and more broadly read or educated" than actual or prospective GBWW owners. They thought the Great Books might be swell for other people, but they didn't need them, thanks. "Marplan essentially concluded that the 'really awares' were too smart to own the Great Books," historian Tim Lacy concludes.

The marketing pros also decided to launch a myriad of "brand extensions," which probably bought the Great Books a decade or two of extra life. First came the ten-volume Great Ideas Program, to which both Benton and Saul Bellow contributed prefaces. Britannica also published *The Great Ideas Today*, *Great Ideas from the Great Books*, and *Gateway to the Great Books*, aimed at children ages 10 to 15. Adler and Hutchins nominally edited

Food for the soul: A 1962 *New Yorker* cartoon.
© THE NEW YORKER COLLECTION, 1962, EVERETT OPIE, FROM CARTOONBANK.COM.
ALL RIGHTS RESERVED.

the *Gateway* and *Great Ideas Today*, which continued publishing until 1998. John Van Doren, Mark Van Doren's other son, went to Chicago in 1969 to take over that series. "I found it was hard to find people who had anything new to say about these disciplines, because they don't change annually, that much," he recalls. "I began to commission articles on substantive issues by people who knew something about them, without claiming that 'This was the year in physics,' or 'This was the year in biology.'"

For a while, the Great Books were important enough to be made fun of, in *New Yorker* cartoons and even in a parody recorded by Chicago's then-new Second City comedy troupe in

1961. The setting was the downtown branch of the University of Chicago, where a motley crew of local citizens wander into a classroom to discuss *Oedipus Rex*. The substitute leader notices that there are very few members in this group. "There were a lot more in the class when we started but *War and Peace* came along and wiped us all out," Scott Peregrine III explains. There are a few period jokes, including this outburst from satisfied Aeschylus reader Belden Stratford: "I had my first catharsis. [I]t was a small one but that's a start."

Adler remained in a state of continuous, promotional overdrive. He wrote a syndicated newspaper column, "Great Ideas from the Great Books," which resulted in a book. His writing ended up in almost every publication in America, although sometimes changes were requested. The associate editor of the *Ladies' Home Journal* generally liked Adler's lengthy encomium to the Books, but had trouble with the first line. "I think the problem which bothers us most is that your first sentence ('You have read Plato's Apology') is improbable," John Morris wrote Adler.

In a P. T. Barnum-esque ploy, Adler arranged to program the Syntopicon onto a UNIVAC computer at the 1962 Seattle World's Fair. In theory, the user would choose one of six subjects, such as "God" or "Liberty," and then place a check mark alongside the names of four of the seventy-four GBWW authors. But the UNIVAC didn't always perform on cue. A young woman wanted to know what Swift, Faraday, Tolstoy, and Freud had to say about the freedom of the individual in society. But in an irate letter that Adler wrote to UNIVAC's John Kamena, he reported that "[t]he print-out she received contained one quotation each from Swift and Freud and the statement 'Among the authors requested only those listed above have discussed the subject of liberty.'" "She was puzzled and angry—and justifiably," Adler wrote, "because she was certain that Tolstoy had discussed liberty." Adler said the printout should have read: "Among the authors requested only those listed above have discussed the subject of the freedom of the individual in society in the works included in 'Great Books of the Western World.'"

Adler even managed to sneak back into the White House. The Kennedy administration held weekly seminars at Hickory Hill, Robert Kennedy's Virginia residence, for "the capital's highest-echelon eggheads," according to the *New York Times*. Inevitably, Adler popped up, lecturing on the Declaration of Independence to Secretary of Defense Robert McNamara, press secretary Pierre Salinger, U.S. Information Agency director Edward R. Murrow, and GBWW pitchman Arthur Schlesinger, Jr., now a White House aide. When the seminar ended, Adler took the occasion to push his reading list of personal favorites: "Locke, Aquinas, Aristotle, and Plato."

Unit sales of the Great Books of the Western World peaked in 1961, and their most profitable year was 1968. But the frenzied publicity and multiple-line brand extensions kept sales going throughout the 1960s and 1970s. Adler wished more than once that he had a piece of the action. He occasionally asked Benton for a one-dollar royalty for each set sold, and Benton just laughed him off. "Nine years of work on the sets and the Syntopicon turned out to be in the end what it was at the beginning—a labor of love," a not very happy-sounding Adler later groused. "One has to have a cushion of wealth," he concluded, jabbing at Benton, "in order to take the risks, and enjoy the advantages, of an entrepreneur."

Over time, the Great Books made plenty of money for the University of Chicago, just as Benton had promised. Britannica, the business Benton had begged the U. of C. trustees to invest in, eventually returned $60 million to Chicago, almost doubling founder John D. Rockefeller's $34 million worth of donations.

The university's official history has this to say about "Benton's folly": "The Great Books of the Western Word was a financial disaster, until it was sold as Hutchins feared it would be—by door-to-door salesmen touting 'culture' to an insecure American middle class."

SEVEN

SECOND VERSE NOT THE SAME AS THE FIRST

MORTIMER ADLER LIVED to see the twenty-first century; not such a great blessing, in retrospect. By the late 1980s, when Adler began plotting a Great Books encore, Hutchins and Benton had been dead for ten and fifteen years, respectively.

Benton passed away in 1973, after a fascinating career in business, politics, and academia. In 1945, President Truman drafted him to be an assistant secretary of state for what Americans would never call propaganda—he oversaw the United States Information Agency, among other things—and Benton was very good at it. He helped create UNESCO, and threw himself gleefully into what soon became an all-out war against the Soviet Union in the marketplace of ideas. Two years later, Truman appointed him to a vacant Connecticut Senate seat, and Benton beat Prescott Bush in the 1950 special election. Benton loved being a U.S. senator, if only for a while. The term lasted just two years, but Benton made the most of it. He was the first and for some time the only man to call for the expulsion of red-baiting Wisconsin senator Joseph McCarthy from the Senate. Benton lost the seat in 1952, which proved to be a landslide year for Eisenhower and the Republicans.

For his part, Hutchins had embarked on a long, gradual, downward trajectory. His perfect marriage to the beautiful sculptress had ended badly. On the one hand, Maude was what might have been called, in another era, neurasthenic. She was frequently ill, and proverbially on the edge of, or actually immersed in, nervous breakdowns. At times, she refused to let her husband leave the house, staging tantrums to keep him at home. On the other hand, through her sculpture, poetry, and fiction writing, Maude was becoming a liberated woman, a term that wouldn't enter the vernacular for another twenty years. Starting in the 1940s, the *New Yorker* printed her poetry, and in 1950, she published the first of five novels, *The Diary of Love*, with the avant-garde New Directions Press. *Diary*—"the tell-all confession of a young girl who grew up with the devil in her flesh!" according to the publisher's blurb—was almost banned in Chicago and was burned in Great Britain, per the order of a prudish magistrate. Hutchins wanted out of the marriage, but Maude wouldn't accede to a divorce. Ignominiously, he had to hide out in hotel rooms and private clubs to force his wife to sue him for desertion in 1948.

To the outside world, Hutchins still projected a glamorous, successful front. In 1949, with twenty years of university experience under his belt, he again appeared on the cover of *Time* magazine, holding forth about the immanence of Truth and Justice, and strewing Hutchins-isms in his wake, e.g. "Compared to Chicago, Yale is a boy's finishing school," or of Chicago, "The faculty does not amount to much, but the president and the students are wonderful."

The magazine proclaimed the 50-year-old Hutchins to be at the top of his game. Only a few intimates knew that his greatest ambitions had gone unfulfilled. Hutchins might have been one of the great Supreme Court justices of the twentieth century, and he

The lion in perpetual summer: Hutchins in Santa Barbara.
DEPARTMENT OF SPECIAL COLLECTIONS, DAVIDSON LIBRARY, UNIVERSITY OF
CALIFORNIA, SANTA BARBARA

longed for a seat on the Court. But his close friend William O. Douglas and others warned him that he would have to earn it, by first serving in political jobs in the Roosevelt administration. Franklin Roosevelt dangled New Deal administrative posts at the Securities and Exchange Commission and the Federal Communications Commission in front of Hutchins, but the haughty educator glaring down from the newsweekly cover turned the president down. Hutchins wanted to play for one team only, his own, and Roosevelt in turn felt no compunction to elevate him to the best job in jurisprudence. At the 1940 Democratic convention in Chicago, Hutchins—the mediagenic "boy wonder"—was boomed for the vice-presidency, but nothing came of it.

Two years after the *Time* cover, Hutchins left the University of Chicago. He landed first at the newly created Ford Foundation, from which great things were expected. "In two years we will change the temper of the country," Hutchins boasted. Not quite. The Ford Foundation of the 1950s was little more than a tax dodge for Henry Ford II, who didn't want his name to become a lightning rod for negative publicity, which Hutchins was serving up by the truckload. Hutchins jousted with the biggest windmills of the time, plunging into the fight against McCarthy and the battle for civil rights. Ford's dealers didn't much fancy Hutchins's crusades, either. Within just a few years, Hutchins bailed out of Ford, taking several million dollars of Henry's money to launch two vanity projects, the brief-lived Fund for the Republic, and then "El Parthenon," the Santa Barbara–based Center for the Study of Democratic Institutions, housed in a phony Greek temple overlooking the Pacific Ocean.

Hutchins would spend almost twenty years at the Center, parading around the grounds in flowery Hawaiian shirts, weaving his Thunderbird amid the avocado groves in the Montecito hills. The idea was to re-create Plato's Academy in America's golden paradise—a year-round, warm-weather Davos, if you will—but the world's greatest minds wouldn't play along. Intellectual celebrities like George Kennan, Aldous Huxley, and Jonas Salk would drop in, and hold forth for Hutchins and the paying visitors for a day or two on airy themes such as "The Public Interest in Education" or "Energy Policies and the International System." But no one stayed for very long. It was, as Joseph Epstein noted, "all of it talk talk talk."

The creation of the atom bomb and the subsequent U.S.-Soviet arms race left Hutchins slightly unhinged. Right after the Hiroshima and Nagasaki hecatombs of 1945, he plunged himself into the world federalist movement and championed the dotty Committee to Frame a World Constitution. There was not going to be a world constitution. Quite the contrary, the world was going the other way, breaking into eastern and western camps, arming to the teeth, and preparing for a forty-five-year-long Cold War. From Santa Barbara, Hutchins organized three international "Pacem in Terris" conferences, in which notables with time on their hands would gather somewhere scenic and bloviate about world peace. His ban-the-bomb work landed him squarely on the screen of the House Un-American Activities Committee, but that was the kind of attention Hutchins welcomed. William F. Buckley called one of the "Pacem" conferences the "Hutchins International Conference to Hate America." It is hard to imagine a day passing when an ironist like Hutchins didn't remember how much his scientific mobilization of the University of Chicago and Dr. Fermi's machinations under the empty bleachers of Stagg Field contributed to the nuclear nightmare that preyed so much on his mind.

Unfortunately, Hutchins lived to see some of his most important educational handiwork undone, almost immediately after he left Chicago. His grand plans had come close to bankrupting the university. Too gleefully, perhaps, Hutchins's successor Lawrence Kimpton told the board of trustees that Chicago had been running a 10 percent operating deficit since 1938. The anti-Hutchins counterrevolution struck quickly. The faculty dismantled the tenth-grade-through-sophomore-year Hutchins College, as it was called, just three years after he left. The plan had been an unmitigated disaster, as undergraduate admissions to the Midway collapsed after the war. "Nobody came," Kimpton explained. Later he would bluntly trash Hutchins in an oral history interview published after his death:

> Every queer and unusual student who disliked athletics and the normal outlets of younger people was attracted to the College. . . . The Great Books course was a joke, and Hutchins knew it was. When I used to kid him about it, how superficial and shallow it was, he would say, "Well, it's better than getting drunk," and I think that's a pretty good summary of it. It certainly made no intellectual contribution.

Perhaps naively, I asked University of Chicago dean John Boyer if there was a portrait or bust of Hutchins in the university's administration building where we met for an interview. "We're not into busts," Boyer replied. Boyer has written several tightly argued monographs on the university's history that are not particularly flattering about Hutchins's contributions to the U. of C., except when praising the president's absolutist defenses of academic freedom.

Adler explained the failure of the Hutchins-Adler experiments to interviewer George Dell in 1976:

> We were moving against the tide, not with it. This country was pragmatic. . . . [T]he whole talk was about how does higher education pay off in jobs and money. We really had ideals and aspirations for education that were thoroughly against the American grain. And I have to add that we were not very ingratiating in the way we proposed. We always laid down the line.

I can't say goodbye to Robert Hutchins without mentioning one of his most admirable qualities: bravery. Yes, he demonstrated physical bravery as an ambulance driver in World War I, but he also exerted great moral courage throughout his life, in a manner we no longer expect or require of university presidents. As a young law professor at Yale, he wrote a brief supporting the Italian anarchists Sacco and Vanzetti. At Chicago, he stood up to the Commies-under-the-bed drugstore magnate Charles Walgreen—the two men ultimately became friends—and he stood up to the Illinois politicians who liked to inveigh against the occasional "pink" U. of C. professor, who might support labor unions or subscribe to the wrong periodical. Hutchins also supported faculty members who had vehemently opposed his reform proposal at the university. His biographers say it was the Oberlin College in him, his unflagging do-goodism that often bled into a cloying self-righteousness.

Hutchins never shed his most unattractive trait: He was easily and often bored, and almost always said so. He once opined that the nuclear age offered a choice: "to be blown up" or "to die of boredom." The U. of C. trustees bored him, he told his father. The student radicals of the 1960s, whom he defended in every public square he could find, bored him. His friend and acolyte Martin Mayer reports that Hutchins's last word was uttered from a hospital bed to his second wife Vesta, who had asked how he was feeling: Hutchins's reply—"Bored." At a lavish fund-raiser intended to save the Santa Barbara Center, Hutchins heard himself praised by the luminaries of the day, including Henry Luce, Norman Cousins, and Adlai Stevenson. Hutchins was moved, but not so moved as to abandon his trademark diffidence: "If I am such a great man," he told the star-studded audience, "why haven't I been able to quit smoking?"

After Hutchins died in 1977, columnist Nicholas von Hoffman wrote: "A remarkable man, Robert Hutchins, perhaps a great one. Unhappily, he won't be missed, he won't even be remembered." Unsparing of others, Hutchins was most unsparing of himself. "I should have died at 35," he told a friend when he was 75.

Two years before his death, Hutchins confided to an interviewer that "my life has been an entire failure." He told the same thing to his former student Sydney Hyman, who became William Benton's biographer: "Everything I've touched, I've failed."

"I said to him, 'Bob, you're crazy, you brought to life a whole generation,'" recalls Hyman, who took the Hutchins-Adler Great Books course at the university in 1935. "We thought of ourselves as the Hutchins Generation. What other college students say something like that?"

By far the best book about Hutchins, and one of the shortest, is *Hutchins' University*, by former U. of C. history professor William McNeill. The president was a "quixotic character" whose "failure was real enough," he writes. But the college's students and teachers "really believed that Chicago's curriculum was the best there was anywhere in the world. For them," McNeill says, "the university was a very special place. Their presence helped to make it so; but so did Hutchins, with his lofty manner, electric wit, and rhetorical extravagances."

"He also made it a very special time, remembered by those who lived through it with awe. Greatness, or something very much like it, walked among us then."

It's not clear who came up with the idea of relaunching the Great Books in 1990. There had been talk of a new edition to honor Adler's 75th birthday in 1977, but cooler heads prevailed. In his second autobiography, Adler attributes the idea to then Britannica chairman Robert Gwinn, and describes his own reaction as "immediate, affirmative and enthusiastic." There is no doubt that Adler careered headlong into the project, not unlike the Imperial Guard rushing to their doom at Waterloo.

The world was not clamoring for a sequel to the "Great Books of the Western World." Benton and Hutchins had long since passed away. The Federal Trade Commission had launched three separate enforcement actions against Britannica, two involving the Great Books. The supersalesmen whom Kenneth Harden unleashed in the 1960s either had been folded back into the Britannica force or drifted west to sell computers, cars, whatever the consumer was hankering for at the moment.

By 1990, the Great Books idea seemed especially shopworn. John Erskine championed the Great Books in reaction to curriculum changes that had taken place one hundred years before. A lot had happened in a hundred years. Forget Forensics! Queer Studies was showing up in the academic mainstream, at major universities such as Duke, Yale, and the University of California. It seemed unlikely that a prominent queer theorist like Eve Kosofsky Sedgwick would be integrating the Great Books into her syllabus anytime soon: "Virtually any aspect of modern Western culture must be, not merely incomplete, but damaged in its central substance to the degree that it does not incorporate a critical analysis of modern homo/heterosexual definition," she wrote in her 1990 book, *Epistemology of the Closet*. At Smith College, the ladies of the Asian Studies Association, the Black Students Alliance, Ekta (South Asian students), the International Students Organization, Korean Students at Smith, Nosotras (Hispanic students), and the Smith African Students Association were staging a sit-in, demanding the college immediately create a multicultural student center. A hundred miles or so to the north, the ultraconservative *Dartmouth Review* was publishing excerpts from Adolf Hitler's call to action, *Mein Kampf.* These weren't the Columbia men in neckties, sitting down with John Erskine and Mark Van Doren to discuss *The Iliad.* These weren't the properly

Jesse Jackson inveighs against Western culture at Stanford.
CHUCK PAINTER / STANFORD NEWS SERVICE

awed University of Chicago undergraduates content to watch President Hutchins blow literal and figurative smoke rings at the end of a seminar table. By 1990, the famous student takeover of Columbia University was twenty-two years in the past. This was not a world the 88-year-old Mortimer Adler was ready to take on.

Did anyone look out the window? Britannica and Adler chose the very moment that the Western canon and "dead white males" in particular were under siege, to sell their "new" collection. It seems comical to recall that Jesse Jackson showed up on the Stanford campus in 1988 to join in the famous, anticanon sloganeering against an unpopular course requirement: "Hey, hey! Ho, ho! Western Culture's got to go!" But he did.

Adler was singularly unsuited to serve as canon fodder. He didn't get the '60s or the '70s or the '80s at all. He had inveighed against "the cult of sensuality, addiction to a life of play and frivolity, the existentialist cop-out which consists in living from day to day with . . . no thought of a good life as a whole" and condemned "over-indulgence in sex," and "psychedelic escapism" in his books and essays.* After the Stanford hijinks, he wrote a long essay decrying multiculturalism. He allowed that cultural pluralism was socially desirable, but . . . don't touch that bookshelf! In learning, he wrote, "[w]hat is desirable is a restricted cultural pluralism; that is, the promotion and preservation of pluralism in all matters of taste, but not in any matters that are concerned with objectively valid truth, either descriptive factual truth or prescriptive normative truth." Translation: Aristotle leaves the syllabus over my dead body.

From the culture's point of view, Adler was a dead white male who had the bad luck to still be alive. To the left, he didn't exist. But the right wing had renounced him as well. In 1988, University of Chicago philosophy professor Allan Bloom hit the jackpot with his jeremiad, *The Closing of the American Mind*, which spent thirty-one weeks on the *New York Times* best-seller list. Bloom deplored the loosey-goosey state of American education, and acknowledged, "Of course, the only serious solution is the one that is almost universally rejected: the good old Great Books approach, in which a liberal education means reading certain generally recognized classic texts." Bloom professed love for the Great Books, but disdained the "cult" founded by his erstwhile University of Chicago colleagues. "It is amateurish," Bloom wrote. "The whole movement has a certain coarse evangelistic tone that is the opposite of good taste." For Adler, he had nothing but contempt:

---

* Regarding Adler the bluestocking, historian Tim Lacy gets off a good line: "This all came from the man Hutchins himself labeled a 'sybarite' and the same Adler who engaged in several extramarital affairs through the 1940s and 1950s."

"Adler's business genius recognized [America's desire for equal access] and made a roaring commercial success out of the Great Books. He was not even concerned about the translations he used, let alone about learning languages."

Adler, the perennial showman and egomaniac, was wounded by Bloom's slight. He called his former colleague "that fool, Allan Bloom" in a series of increasingly bitter interviews. In Adler's papers, there is a draft of a speech called "Setting the Record Straight," outlining the high points of his rebuttal to Bloom, which he would merchandise to anyone who would listen.

"Because of the serious defects, inexcusable negligence, and downright errors in Mr. Bloom's treatment of great books, democracy and philosophical truth, I am impelled to set the record straight," Adler fumed. "I would be less than candid were I not to add at once that I am also motivated by his one reference to me. Its insinuation that my only concern with great books was making money out of the sale of the Great Books of the Western World, published in 1952 . . . is an *infra dig* slur." The 86-year-old Adler pointed out that he had been teaching the Great Books with John Erskine before Allan Bloom was born: "Allan Bloom is either inexcusably ignorant of all the work we did, which he should have gracefully applauded; or worse, he intentionally ignored it in order to give the impression that his own recommendation that the great books be read by college students was an educational innovation by him."

On *Firing Line*, William F. Buckley taunted his old pal by reciting Bloom's formidable sales figures. Adler jumped at the bait. "[Bloom] and his master, Leo Strauss, teach the Great Books as if they were teaching the truth. But when I teach them, I want to understand the errors," Adler railed, as if public television viewers had the faintest idea who the German-born philosopher

Leo Strauss was, or what errors Adler was talking about. "They indoctrinate their students with the 'truth' they find in the books," Adler continued. "Strauss reads Plato and Aristotle as if it was all true, i.e., women are inferior, and some men are destined to be slaves."

While inveighing against Bloom, Adler was preparing to launch the new, revised 1990 edition of the Britannica Great Books. The selection process was déjà vu all over again. Again, Adler convened a board of experts, most of them plucked from his hip pocket, like Columbia's seemingly ageless Jacques Barzun, former *Saturday Review* editor Norman Cousins, Harvard economist John Kenneth Galbraith, and others. And again, there was the exchange of memos among board members lobbying for personal favorites: "Mr. Cousins agreed strongly with those of you who wanted Flaubert, but that still left Flaubert with only 4 votes. He objected to dropping Fielding, saying that he did not know how one could choose between Fielding and Austen, that the absence of either one would cause comment."

The changes were underwhelming indeed. The committee voted four Great Books authors off the island: Apollonius of Perga, and his "Conics" ("I regretted dropping the 'Conics'"— Adler); Joseph Fourier's "Analytical Theory of Heat"; Laurence Sterne's *Tristram Shandy*; and Henry Fielding's *Tom Jones*. "I thought we were wrong in dropping Fielding," Adler wrote, and couldn't refrain from adding, "And I thought we were wrong in adding Voltaire's *Candide* . . . *Candide* is not a great book."

Into the gaps left in the original fifty-four-volume set, the committee inserted many names left on the table when Hutchins, Erskine, Adler, Buchanan & Co. were doing their horse-trading in 1943 and 1944. John Calvin finally made the cut, as did François Rabelais, Molière, Racine, Voltaire, Diderot, Kierkegaard,

Nietzsche, de Toqueville, Balzac, Jane Austen, George Eliot, Henrik Ibsen, Charles Dickens, and Mark Twain. As a sop to modernity, the committee added six new volumes of twentieth-century works to the Great Books, canonizing eleven new scientists, seven new philosophers, seven new social scientists, and twenty new practitioners of "imaginative literature."* Along with Austen and Eliot, Willa Cather and Virginia Woolf were the sole women to be included in the Great Books. No blacks or Hispanics appeared on the list.

Britannica dutifully prepared its sales force for the inevitable questions. A 1990 marketing memo noted that glaring exclusions of most women and all people of color "will be the hottest critical commentary when the set is released—and we welcome it! We expect much controversy. . . . [T]his kind of coverage will do much to bring 'Great Books' back as a topic for debate once again."

It gets worse. The anonymous briefer continues: "We have also answered an objection of more recency—namely, where are the women? We *have* come a long way, baby, and thus we have Jane and George, as well as Willa Cather and Virginia Woolf in the 20th century."

To which one can only say: Ouch.

The formal talking points explain that "we did not deliberately select Great Books on the basis of an author's nationality, religion or subject area. Neither did we select Great Books on the basis of gender or race."

Preparing for the fancy kick-off, black-tie banquet event at the Library of Congress, festooned with such conservative celebrities as William F. Buckley and Gertrude Himmelfarb,

---

* The complete list of twentieth-century additions appears in my (Randomly Annotated) Great Books list, at the end of this book.

Adler thought it would be best not to broach what he called the "affirmative action" issue. Britannica's top PR man, Norman Braun, counseled otherwise: "The issue will come up. To omit it from the list of questions and responses may invite press accusations of editorial racism, etc."

It did come up. At the ceremony during which Adler and Britannica boss Gwinn presented a complete, $1,400 set to Librarian of Congress James Billington, a Library staffer named Prosser Gifford ventured that "[s]urely the great Latin American authors are part of the 'great conversation.'" Gifford, the only dissonant voice that appears in the Library's account of the meeting, also noted that "the great conversation of ideas in the Western tradition is not limited to people who live in the North Atlantic" areas of the world. Silence, groundling! Adler scoffed at the "irrelevance of these criticisms."

But scoffing takes you only so far. Henry Louis Gates, Jr., then a professor at Duke, got the ball rolling in an interview with the *New York Times*: "It distresses me that the editors couldn't find more women and people of color to include in this new edition. . . . Obviously, there's still a 'whites only' sign on what precisely constitutes a great thinker." The *Chicago Tribune*'s John Blades wrote, "The absence of black writers from the expanded library of classics seems certain to rile an increasingly vocal body of critics who maintain that the standard literary texts (or canon) slight or ignore the work of women and various religions and ethnic groups." Blades quoted Adler as insisting that "there are no 'Great Books' by black writers before the 1955 cutoff. 'There are good books by blacks—about 10—that are worth reading for one or two ideas, and they are in the Syntopicon.' [Adler] says the debate over the canon is 'Utter nonsense. Rubbish, rubbish, rubbish. . . . This is the canon, and it's not revisable.'"

This is precisely what the ever-more-addled Adler was telling interviewers around the country. Blacks "didn't write any good books," he told the *Los Angeles Times*. If there are no Latino authors, it's because "[selection committee member] Octavio Paz didn't recommend any." Too Eurocentric? If "[Asians] came to the West, they better learn Western culture. If they want to stay Japanese, they should stay in Japan."

In the same month as the launch, Adler told *Jet* magazine's primarily black audience: "I think probably in the next century there will be some Black that writes a great book, but there hasn't been any so far." In a letter to Adler, the president of the school council of Chicago's Goldblatt Elementary School quoted from the *Jet* article, and said: "The racism implicit in these remarks is rivaled only by their untruth." William Johnson, president of the Urban League of Rochester, sent a letter to Britannica executive Gwinn, with a copy to the Urban League's national president: "I have a question: Can you clarify the criteria by which writers, thinkers and scientists are selected for your publication? Perhaps then I will better understand why important themes—oppression, racism, equality, freedom, history, culture, identity—are reflected only in the works of Eurocentric writers, thinkers and scientists." Johnson added: "Until this error is corrected, I cannot and will not recommend that anyone purchase these volumes."

Mortimer Adler lived on eleven more years, in progressively failing health, until his death in 2001. He continued to teach seminars to the business "bozos," as he called them behind their backs, at the Aspen Institute. Since the early 1980s, he had been promoting an elementary school version of the Great Books, called the Paideia Proposal (*paideia* means "education" in Greek), that had pretty much run out of gas by the time of his death. For much of his life, up until 1995, he published or edited a book a year. Like Hutchins's, some of Adler's later efforts flirted with absurdity. He published an Aquinas-like "proof" that God created the cosmos. He took to calling latter-day philosophers like Ludwig Wittgenstein "ignoramuses," scoring their insufficient appreciation of Aristotle.

Although he had converted to Catholicism shortly before his death, Adler's memorial service took place at the high Episcopal church he frequented while living in Chicago, St. Chrysostom's on the Gold Coast. His friend Max Weissman read the Twenty-Third Psalm. Adler's first son Mark also read, and Mark Van Doren's son Charles delivered the last of three eulogies. Charles, a former lecturer at Columbia, does not like to talk about the quiz show scandal that effectively ended his life in polite society, but he mentioned it at Adler's service: "And then there came the time when I fell down, face down in the mud, and he picked me up, brushed me off, and gave me a job."

Adler did give Van Doren a behind-the-scenes job at Britannica, after his best friend's son had suffered national disgrace. "He saved Charlie's life," Sydney Hyman says. "Everyone knows that." "He was very loyal to people," Charles's brother John recalled. "He had all sorts of philosopher pals on some sort of retainer to Britannica. But people were not loyal to him."

Adler never had an academic job after he left the University of Chicago in 1946. He was generally unwelcome on American campuses, with the possible exception of St. John's, and lived off his Britannica work, occasional grants for "philosophical" inquiry, his Aspen seminars, and his frantic publishing schedule. "You won't find his name in a dictionary of philosophers," John Van Doren continued. "There is not a single mention of him in the most recently published *Dictionary of 20th Century American Philosophy*. He doesn't exist. I think it's a great pity." "He made people believe that they could think seriously about ideas outside the university academic structure," says Howard Zeiderman, a tutor at St. John's. "He did something that was terrifically important, because there is a hunger in this country on the part of people who want to think. For better or worse, he tried to address that."

Like Hutchins at the end of his life, Adler, too, judged himself harshly. Charles Van Doren told me about one of the last conversations he had with Adler, who was speaking by telephone from his retirement home in San Mateo, California: "He said: 'You know, Charles, everything that I've done has been forgotten. My life has been a failure.' And I said: 'Oh no, Mort, of course that's not true,' and I repeated that thought in every way. And he said: 'Don't. Don't. What I'm saying is true.'"

I told Van Doren that Hutchins had said much the same thing, and I remarked that extremely intelligent, vain men are sometimes overly self-critical. Van Doren corrected me: "No, I think they were both right."

EIGHT

THE PEOPLE
OF THE BOOK

W HERE DID THOSE 1 million sets of Great Books go? Hundreds if not thousands went to libraries, quite possibly never to be opened a second time, after a staffer dutifully affixed an *ex libris* sticker inside the front cover of all fifty-four volumes. Thousands became adornments, either in corporate offices or in the kind of living rooms that functioned as imagined "salons," spaces so tidy and vacuumed that family members never dared set foot in them. And thousands of copies, perhaps tens of thousands, were actually read, and had an enormous impact on the lives of the men, women, and children who read them.

In the course of a conversation about NCAA Division II football, I mentioned to University of Massachusetts journalism professor Ralph Whitehead, Jr., that I was writing about the Great Books. The Great Books! Whitehead grew up in Chicago, where his mother sometimes saw Robert Hutchins practice his fly casting in the lagoon at Washington Park, and in Appleton, Wisconsin, where his father worked as an executive for Kimberly-Clark. His parents participated in Great Books discussion groups and owned many of the inexpensive paperbacks published by the Great Books Foundation. The books were read, and not just by the grown-ups. Included in our copious e-mail exchanges, here is Whitehead's account of his early encounters with greatness, lying on the living room floor of his family's tiny apartment, where he slept on a bed that folded out from the wall:

I was born in 1943, and by the time I was five or six my dad had told me, largely in his own words, the stories of *The Iliad* and *The Odyssey*, and then began actually to read to me from *Robinson Crusoe*—not every paragraph, as I later realized when I read it for myself years later, but the parts that speak to a boy's sense of adventure and some of the parts about how Crusoe went about building a dwelling and getting food.

It was at some point after we'd gone through *Robinson Crusoe* that my dad suggested that I look at *Gulliver's Travels* and try to read it for myself. By then, I had already heard about Gulliver and the Lilliputians, and since the book doesn't begin with the voyage to Lilliput, I was thrown off at the start. I'd already made my way through the dialect in *Huckleberry Finn* and saw the old-fashioned prose in *Gulliver* as a similar challenge. It took me hours just to decipher three or four pages of the book. I knew nothing of the original satiric objects of the book, of course, and read it strictly as a ripping yarn.

I clearly remember that I opened up the Aeschylus book and the Sophocles book repeated times. Because they were books of plays, there was a lot of white space on the pages, and I kept figuring that this would make them easy to read. But I never could succeed in figuring out what the hell was going on. In time, this proved to help me with the book of Plato. The Socratic dialogues (I had no idea then that this is what they were called) also had a lot of white space, and I was actually able to understand them a bit—not a lot, but better than the plays. This told me something that I was able to act on when I was a number of years older: Philosophy sounds like it's hard, but Plato is surprisingly easy to read.

Whitehead later attended Lawrence College (now Lawrence University) in Appleton, where President Nathan Pusey—a future Harvard president—had instituted a Great Books–like "core" program for first-year students, called Freshman Studies. For the young Whitehead, the reading list was déjà vu all over again: Plato, *Antigone*, *The Communist Manifesto*, and *The Prince*, admixed with some of the more modern readings that Adler shoehorned into the Great Books second edition: *Heart of Darkness*, Chekhov, and so on.

The Great Books paid off in spades in Whitehead's senior year, when he traveled to New York with the Lawrence team to face down the Virginia Military Academy in the popular national TV show "General Electric College Bowl." The team attended a play at the American Place Theater, and Whitehead still remembers spotting the intellectual celebrities of the day: "Orson Bean was sitting in front of us, making out with a young woman. During the intermission, we went out into the lobby, and there were Ralph Ellison and Robert Lowell and Allen Tate catching a smoke."

VMI had been drilling. Footloose in the big city, the self-confident Lawrence team had been "chilling." "There wasn't a lot of time for practice," Whitehead explains. The cadets crushed Lawrence in several practice rounds, but when the klieg lights came on, Whitehead and his friends won a surprise victory, and then went on to defeat four more adversaries, before being forcibly retired.

During the contests, Whitehead remembers,

[a] number of my answers were things I somehow dredged up from my earlier acquaintance with the Great Books. As it happened, there was a question about Aeschylus. There was a question about *Moby Dick*, a question about Thoreau, a question about Engels.

At one point, the host, Robert Earle, showed my team a painting of two men dressed in classical garb. One was pointing up, the other was pointing either straight or down (I can't recall!). The question was something like: Can you identify each of the philosophers in this painting? Because a copy of Plato had been in my home for 15 years, it was pretty easy to say that Plato, the philosophical idealist, was the guy who was pointing up, and so the guy who was pointing flat or down would have to be the more empirically-minded Aristotle.

"Whatever I was able to contribute was mainly thanks to the Great Books," Whitehead says.

The late critic Ian Hamilton wrote a wonderful book called *The Keepers of the Flame*. It describes the devotees, the fanatics, the misguided relatives, the people left behind by great talents, who fancied themselves serving their idols long after the great flames had been extinguished. Hamilton offers several examples, the most notorious being Rupert Brooke's overbearing mother and executor, known as "The Ranee," and Robert Louis Stevenson's widow Fanny Osbourne, who devoted their natural lives to protecting their dear and departed from scandalous memoirists and former lovers hawking troves of compromising letters. An updated version of Hamilton's book would have to include flame tender Max Weismann, a dapper, 72-year-old businessman turned Great Books devotee.

The Great Books changed many lives, and Max Weismann's was one of them. A high school dropout whose father wanted him to become a house painter, Max has instead become a character, an icon of a bygone Chicago occasionally stumbled upon by newspaper feature writers. When I met him, he was still holding court at the Pump Room of the Ambassador East Hotel, which, many years ago, was a place to be seen. Bicoastal celebrities traveling by train would overnight at the Ambassador, and the photographers and gossip columnists working for the big newspapers and syndicates would visit the Pump Room most evenings to snap a picture and grab a few harmless quotes. "The arrival of these celebrities by train is a sign that they desire to be interviewed," A. J. Liebling noted sardonically, "since otherwise they would simply fly over." These days, it is a celebrity graveyard, with photographs of Frank Sinatra, Eddie Albert, and Gig Young still adorning the walls. Max, who claims the title of "honorary president of the Pump Room," notes that the hotel still has a Frank Sinatra suite: "In Chicago, this is the only place he stayed."

Max lives in the neighborhood, Chicago's Gold Coast, near St. Chrysostom's, where he spoke at Mortimer Adler's memorial service. Max was impeccably dressed in a tweed sport coat and dark turtleneck, and as we talked he nursed his favorite drink, a Grey Goose essence of orange vodka, and smoked Benson & Hedges menthol cigarettes. Since our encounter, Chicago has banned smoking in bars that serve food, so Max now smokes on the street, alongside the Ambassador's doorman, whom he has known forever.

Max was a young design engineer, a 1950s-era motorcyclist first and a young husband and father second, living in Milwaukee, Wisconsin, when a friend convinced him to attend a Great Books seminar on *The Communist Manifesto* at the public library. "Khrushchev was in power, it seemed like a chance to see what communism was all about. My friend had made a mistake, the discussion was actually about Plato's 'Apology,' which we hadn't read. I had never heard of Socrates before," Weismann explains. "I had a religious epiphany. I owe that discussion leader everything. I realized what an ignorant person I had been. It changed my life, every day, to this day that we are sitting here." Weismann asked the discussion leader, "Whose idea was this? And he said, 'Somebody named Mortimer Adler.'"

Max became a different person. "I sold my motorcycles and started buying books. I realized that I wanted to be a philosopher and teacher just like Mortimer Adler. My wife thought I had lost my mind." He even bought a set of the Great Books of the Western World for $595, which, he reminds me, "was a lot of money in those days." Professionally, Weismann apprenticed himself to an architect and learned the construction engineering trade. He also made a tidy sum of money patenting a color printing process, but he explains that "I was never into architecture—that was just a way to do philosophy. I wanted to make money only because I wanted to do what Adler was doing and I wanted to work with him."

And that is exactly what he did.

Weismann moved to Chicago, and befriended Adler. Max says he and Adler dined together every evening in the Pump Room when his mentor still lived in the neighborhood. (Adler moved to San Mateo, California, in 1995.) As Adler started to lose his vision, Weismann says he began to handle some of the master's correspondence: "That is how close we were." In 1990, the two men founded the Center for the Study of the Great Ideas. A $20 membership still entitles you to the weekly e-journal "The Great Ideas Online" and the quarterly publication, *Philoso-*

phy Is Everybody's Business. For $45, you also receive "Personal philosophical and educational consultation, access to Dr. Adler's books, articles, and video programs, [and] participation in The Great Ideas Discussion Forums and Seminars."

The Center exists on the Internet, and on the hard disc of Max's iMac computer. It is a digital shrine to the memory of Adler. Every June 28, Max sends an e-mail message to all of his members, reminding them that "[t]oday is the anniversary of Mortimer Adler's departure from our midst."

The Center hosts online discussion forums that don't seem to be very well attended, and several times a year Max himself leads an online Great Ideas seminar—not a Great Books seminar—where "we do not discuss books per se, but rather the ideas and issues found in them." They attract between twenty and thirty participants. The Center also engages in e-commerce, and is the go-to site for the handful of people, like me, who might want to buy DVDs of all of Adler's appearances on William F. Buckley's TV show *Firing Line*, or any book that Adler ever wrote. Max says he has sold "millions" of books, tapes, and discs off of the website, but doesn't want to discuss specific numbers. When I inquired about copyrights, Weismann told me that Adler had granted the nonprofit Center access to all of his materials. He declines to say how many members he has.

And every day, he tends the flame. "I'm digitizing everything Adler ever wrote," Weismann says. "I would like to write a Syntopicon of his work."

I attended several official Great Books events while researching this book, one of them a weekend retreat in Mystic, Connecticut. In March 2007, about a hundred people converged on the Mystic

Hilton for two and a half days. Most of them knew one another from previous Great Books events. A core of perhaps thirty or forty make an annual tour of the major Great Books events, from the Chicago Great Books Week (now just a weekend) in May, to the longer Classical Pursuits seminar in Toronto, and finally to the well-attended summer Great Books week at Colby College in Maine.

Great Books people are great socializers, so I had no trouble making friends at the bar under the rescued buoys and thick hawsers in the faux-nautically themed Soundings Lounge of the Mystic Hilton. I have the Great Books bar scene to thank for meeting Karen Pizarro, a parochial school principal from Princeton, New Jersey, who was sitting in the Lounge with a couple of friends, nursing a drink and talking about books, of course. Karen was funny. Practically the first story she told was how she and her mother met Mortimer Adler and Clifton Fadiman at the Hotel Jerome bar in Aspen in the mid-1950s. "They were very flirtatious," Karen recalled. "My mother was this gorgeous redhead, and when they invited us over to their table for a long conversation, I thought that quite an ordinary occurrence, since Adler was a household name in our home." Her brother Tom, a young boy at the time, remembered the scene clearly when I spoke with him later: "Adler was hitting on my mother."

Karen and Tom had grown up in an extremely unusual household captained by their father Thomas Hyland, whose two main interests in life, according to his son, were "reading Great Books and killing Japs." Though Thomas was born poor, his stellar academic and athletic record at Denver Cathedral High School won him a scholarship to Columbia in 1938. He had to hitchhike to Manhattan's Upper West Side because he couldn't afford a bus or train ticket.

Pilot Thomas Hyland, who loved "reading Great Books and killing Japs."
COURTESY OF THE HYLAND FAMILY

Hyland fell under the spell of Columbia's legendary Classical Civilization course, a core curriculum created at almost exactly the same time as John Erskine's General Honors program. "Contemporary Civilization turned my Dad's life around," his son recalls. "He left for Columbia as a devout Catholic, and the school just shattered his world. He came back a dedicated Marxist who later led union strikes and met with Jimmy Hoffa." Hyland studied hard and also worked full-time, to supplement his scholarship and to send money back to his family. The effort overwhelmed him. He left Columbia after two years to return to work in a Denver bank.

Just a few months before America entered World War II, Hyland joined the navy and became a pilot. He was a much-decorated ace, flying B-24 Liberators in the Pacific theater, and was credited with shooting down twelve enemy planes. His own bomber was shot down twice. His crewmen, whose lives he saved on several occasions, worshipped him. "We were led by the Great Tom Hyland, in my opinion the best P.P.C. [Pilot-Patrol Plane Commander] to fly a PBY4–1," bow gunner Walter Bryant recalled after the war. "He always passed credit around. He never used the word 'I,' his word was 'we.'" Hyland's son Tom remembers how much Thomas loved fighting: "When he found out the war was over, he cried. He didn't want it to end."

After the war, Hyland began a thirty-year career as a pilot for United Airlines, a job he adored for one reason: It afforded him time to read. "He said flying a plane was just like being a cab driver," Pizarro told me. "He liked the job because it gave him all kinds of time to read the Great Books." He never talked politics in the cockpit, and he never discussed literature, either. "He had no respect for pilots," Tom says. "He said they were the dumbest sons of bitches that ever walked." But flying had its perquisites. One day, before taking off from San Francisco, flight attendants summoned Hyland from the cockpit to deal with a frightened passenger. It turned out to be John Steinbeck, who needed several drinks to quell his fear of flying. Hyland thought the author of *The Grapes of Wrath* was America's greatest living writer, and told him so. Flattery calms all turbulence, emotional and atmospheric. Whenever Steinbeck needed to fly cross-country, he phoned Hyland to learn his schedule, and planned his flights accordingly.

Hyland was the perfect citizen-reader who figured prominently in the imaginations of Robert Hutchins and Mortimer Adler, but less so in the real world. Back from Columbia, he wooed his bride-to-be with talk of books and ideas. "Our whole family used to watch the quiz shows, '21,' and 'The $64,000 Question,' and what was so awesome was that my Mom and Dad got all the answers right without cheating," Tom recalls. "As far back as I can remember, books were everywhere, books were talked about constantly. From my earliest memory they were both hammering home the idea of the Great Books." Did they own the Britannica set? "Yes, we had several copies of those," Tom says. "They're rather forbidding, they are something you think of monks reading in monasteries in the Middle Ages."

"Home was our school," Karen Pizarro remembers. "School was dull. When the teachers would say, 'You need to go to the library and get a certain book,' I would just look on my Dad's shelves. I didn't enter a library until I was an adult. He encouraged us not only to read, but to memorize the Declaration of Independence, the Preamble to the Constitution, the Bill of Rights, and the Gettysburg Address. He thought that everyone had an unconquerable mind." Her father gave away a fair portion of his pilot's salary to family members who needed the money for school or college. His one extravagance was books. "I remember the sound of the hammer going all the time, with him building bookshelves," Pizarro says. "At one point, when the books began to replace necessary furniture like beds, one of my brothers built stacks of shelves, and my sister catalogued the books using the Dewey decimal system!"

When he died in 2003, Hyland had amassed a library of 63,000 books. In his will, he asked for them to be redistributed in a three-day estate sale, with paperbacks priced at ten cents and hardcovers at three dollars. Maybe news was slow on the weekend of January 31, 2004, but five Denver television stations covered the sale, broadcasting pictures of hundreds of buyers lined up outside of Hyland's split-level home to carry off bagfuls and, in some cases, rolling containers full of books. "It really does look like a library," gushed reporter Karen Tilley in a live shot for Channel 7.

Hyland's children and grandchildren honored his last request: to be buried with a copy of Adler's 1940 best-seller, *How to Read a Book*. Hyland's son Tom, a self-styled "urban monk" who devotes his life to learning, still swears by *How to Read a Book* and calls Adler "one of the greatest Americans who ever lived." Even if—or perhaps because—he made a pass at Hyland's mother. "It's a book I still read," says Tom. "I made certain all three of my children read it. They have thanked me again and again for doing it."

His sister Karen reports that she has eighty-five copies of Adler's best-seller in her home, most of them gifts from her father. She parts company with her brother when discussing the merits of Adler's famous tome. "It's an awful book," she says. "It's one of the worst books ever written. If we brought our boyfriends home, they would read it just to impress us."

But . . . she is willing to follow Adler, and her father, into the next world: "I have sworn that I'll read it from cover to cover in case I meet my father in the great beyond."

There is a Noble Savage myth underlying the pedagogy of the Great Books. It was best embodied in the spirit of the 1921 People's Institute, the myth that the longshoreman toting pallets, or the housewife at her ironing board, could commune with Epictetus and Galileo just as easily as the college undergraduate.

So it was no accident that Adler seized on this astonishing 1985 letter from David Call, a fan in Springville, Utah, who had seen him on public television:

Dear Mr. Adler,

I am writing in behalf [sic] of a group of construction workers (mostly, believe it or not, plumbers!) who have finally found a teacher worth listening too [sic]. . . . We have been studying your books for over a year now and have put together a sizeable library of your writings.

I am sure that it is just due to our well-known ignorance as trades-men that not a single one of us had ever heard of you until one Sunday afternoon we were watching public television and Bill Moyers came on with his show Six Great Ideas. We listened intensely and soon became addicted and have been ever since. We never knew a world of ideas existed.

Naturally, Adler entered into correspondence with Call, who soon revealed that he and his brother had signed up for a philosophy class at the University of Utah and had taken to wearing "Great Ideas" baseball caps on their construction site. He also offered Adler an example of what it is like to philosophize on a construction site:

Several days ago my brother and I were discussing free-will and determinism within the hearing distance of a group of brick layers. They were busily laying their brick but could not help but overhear our philosophical arguments. Finally, one of the brick layers could take it no longer and shouted over to us: "I've got a philosophical question!" Surprised, we inquired as to what it was, to which he responded, "What is your philosophy on getting a good orgasm?"

Adler kept a folder of his correspondence with Call, whom he dubbed "the philosophical plumber," and he boasted about the relationship in *Time* magazine and in *A Second Look in the Rearview Mirror*, his second autobiography. "He kind of adopted me as an icon," Call now remembers. Adler sent him and his colleagues several hundred dollars' worth of books.

Call was a committed Mormon, and a very serious adept of Adler's teaching. Just a few months into their relationship, he wrote:

> *P.S. If you and I die, Dr. Adler, and if we go to hell, I'll look you up and together we will boot out the devil and every other moral relativist and we'll turn hell into an absolute heaven!*

This postscript to another letter could not have found favor with Adler, a self-confessed egomaniac:

> *P.S. Just the other day I asked an individual who I was doing some work for if he knew who Mortimer Adler was; he said, "Isn't that a cartoon character?" to which I quickly responded "No, I didn't say 'little Abner' I said Mortimer Adler!" . . . I can't believe your [sic] not better known or praised, you certainly deserve it.*

Call sent Adler a paper he had written for his philosophy class, a paper that earned him a verbal reprimand and a C-plus, whereas all his previous grades had been A's or A-minuses. The essay, "Heterosexuals—the Silent Majority," argued, based on Call's readings of Lincoln and the Founding Fathers, that homosexuals are falsely trying to assert "natural rights" in contemporary America. Ultimately it devolved into an anti-homosexual manifesto:

> In the name of human freedom; in the name of liberty not licence; and in the name of public morality and the democratic

process, let us meet this challenge and not allow sexual degradation to stand alongside of all the noble causes that we Americans have fought so long and hard for. Let us let the rest of the world know that we Americans stand for Liberty and not licence!

There is no trace of a reply from Adler.

David Call still lives in Springville, where I reached him by telephone. He eventually finished Brigham Young University and retired from plumbing. Now in his late 50s, he has embarked on a new career that combines multilevel marketing with inspirational speaking. He is a mile-a-minute talker with an Adlerian gift of gab. It took all of my will power not to buy a $399 blender from Team Everest, his flashy website. He remembers Adler fondly and marvels at his mentor's astonishing longevity: "He never exercised or did anything, and he outlived everyone around him. I really appreciated what he did for me."

NINE

EPICTETUS AT THE CASH REGISTER

CHICAGO AND COLUMBIA

WHILE WORKING ON THIS BOOK, I spent many mornings at the Medici Café on the University of Chicago campus, postponing my inevitable return to Chicago's imposing, neo-Brutalist Regenstein Library, and to the wild disarray of Mortimer Adler's fascinating, uncatalogued personal files. Occasionally, a Chicago undergraduate wandered into the Medici wearing a maroon T-shirt emblazoned with the university's unofficial motto: "Where Fun Goes to Die." Other versions of the T-shirt proclaim "The Circle of Hell That Dante Never Imagined" or depict a dinosaur trampling on a stick man. The dinosaur is labeled "UC" and the stick man, "your soul."

The undergraduate self-pity is, of course, misplaced. Chicago, imbued with Robert Hutchins's ancient disdain for the slacking "college men" who littered the Ivy League campuses of his day, is in business to educate students, not to coddle them. While it is true that the school dismantled Hutchins's brief-lived, four-year-long Great Books undergraduate experiment decades ago, it remains one of the very few major colleges committed to a "core" curriculum for its undergraduates. What that means at Chicago is that roughly one-third of an undergraduate's time is spent taking courses prescribed by the university. When Chicago was embroiled in its widely publicized "core wars" at the end of the 1990s—inevitably, the U. of C. was cutting back on its Western Civilization requirements—Kurt White, a senior from Birmingham, Michigan, told the *New York Times*: "It may be harder to get into Harvard, but it's harder to get out of here, and I'm proud of that. This is one of the very last places that has a rigorous curriculum." It was true under Hutchins, and it's somewhat true today.

Chicago's storied "core" has been watered down considerably since the young Susan Sontag and Katharine Graham grappled with the Western classics. After Hutchins's departure, Chicago's formidable anthropologists and cultural historians pushed back against the Aristotelian-Medieval core, mixing Asian and African cultural studies into the stew of required classes. The 1998 "core wars" contributed to the departure of President Hugo Sonnenschein, who dared to cut back the number of required courses, in part to free up undergraduates' limited time on campus, and in part to make the campus a place where fun could go to flourish, not to die.

As part of a larger "rebranding" of the university, Sonnenschein, an economist, sought to reduce the core from about one-half to about one-third of the undergraduate curriculum, and tinkered with the college's Western Civilization courses. The resulting outcry might have been predicted. The faculty, adequately forewarned, reacted much less strongly than some conservative alumni, who formed a pressure group called Concerned Friends of the University of Chicago, and threatened to withhold their donations. The Princeton-based, conservative National Association of Scholars, not to be denied a Halley's comet–like opportunity for publicity, issued a press release quoting NAS president

Stephen Balch: "It is truly depressing to observe a steady abandonment of the University of Chicago's once imposing undergraduate core curriculum, which for so long stood as the benchmark of content and rigor among American academic institutions."

At the height of the nonshooting war, Sonnenschein defended his policies at a stormy meeting attended by students and faculty in Hutchinson Commons, the ersatz-medieval, wood-paneled student center. Someone even shouted "Long Live Hutchins!" from the back of the room, and two students seized the opportunity to sell CDs of their humorous song, "The End of the Core as We Know It," a parody of a famous REM hit. But within months the campus settled down, the core changed, and Sonnenschein later abandoned the Chicago presidency and returned to the Economics Department. "It's a non-issue now," says Dean John Boyer, who was partly responsible for implementing some of the curriculum changes.

Today, Chicago is the very model of a modern university, and when I suggested to Boyer that one could get through the modern U. of C. without ever reading a Great Book of the Western World, he harrumphed. But it's true. Navigating the Chinese menu–like core course requirements in the Humanities, Civilization Studies, and Social Sciences isn't easy, but I found a path that skirted the heavy lifting of Plato, Aristotle, and Hobbes. The Humanities rubric, for instance, offers a course called "Reading Cultures: Collection, Travel, Exchange." "It is total flake garbage," says a professor who helped design the course as one of Chicago's "young and the restless" academicians in the 1990s. "It was a serious joke, like diving into a bowl of viscous nothing. They were watching Philippine films and reading second-rate literature." To be fair, "Reading Cultures" now watches *Citizen Kane*, and includes readings from what sounds like a bona fide, Britannica-approved

Great Book, Ovid's "Metamorphoses." (Although John Erskine taught Ovid in General Studies, the Latin poet was never even suggested for the Great Books, which included only "epic" poems by Chaucer, Dante & Co.) Humanities also offers a notorious core cycle called "Media Aesthetics," which one undergraduate calls "a great course if you don't like to read books." "We teach Browning and Wyatt alongside Cindy Sherman and Chuck Close," Humanities professor James Chandler wrote in the *University of Chicago Magazine.* They also teach *Vertigo, The Conversation,* and, yes, *Citizen Kane.*

It is harder to slip past the Social Science requirement and avoid the likes of Marx, Weber, and Adam Smith, but if that's your aim, take "Mind": "This course focuses on the issue of what is innate versus what is learned, the development of thought in children, and the logic of causal, functional, and evolutionary explanations," the catalog explains. Chicago has serious mathematics and foreign-language requirements, and it also forces undergrads to take science courses designed to force liberal arts majors' noses into the muck of empirical inquiry. No one seems to know if Chicago's required core is a selling point or a stumbling block for recruiting the A-list high school seniors all colleges covet. It is certainly no longer a lightning rod for campus dissent. "I like the core," says student Tim Murphy. "You're guaranteed a balanced education if you come here."

Ironically, the University of Chicago does still teach the Great Books, Hutchins-Adler style, but not to its students. For over sixty years, the university's extension college, the Graham School, has been offering its Basic Program, a four-year-long adult seminar with a reading list that flew directly from Mortimer Adler's famous Royal typewriter to the Graham catalog:

Year One

Autumn: Sophocles, Plato, Dostoyevsky

Winter: Herodotus, Aeschylus, Aristotle

Spring: Machiavelli, Hobbes, Kant, Conrad, Bible,
Kierkegaard

Clare Pearson, a product of Chicago's Committee on Social
Thought—the U. of C.'s high-minded parking lot for such talents
as Saul Bellow, Leo Strauss, and Allan Bloom—administers the
Basic Program, which she calls "an anomaly in continuing education. It is the heart of a UC education, of the old school." The
Program is popular, attracting between 400 and 450 students each
year, about a quarter of whom will earn a two-year or four-year
Certificate in the Liberal Arts. The clientele are not the great un-
washed of Adler and Fadiman's People's Institute. Their average
age is 55, and 65 percent of them hold graduate degrees. "It's not
really a populist program," Pearson explains.

Just as in the university's core curriculum, U. of C. senior and
junior faculty teach in the Basic Program. At the Graham School,
they use John Erskine's old "shared inquiry" methodology, albeit
with only one teacher in the classroom. No one can afford two
these days. The Basic Program is decidedly Old School. There is
a quote from Robert Hutchins—"The great books do not yield
up their secrets to the immature"—plastered front and center on
the Program catalog, and there are no "core wars" here. "We review the program every year, but the changes aren't terribly significant," Pearson says. "Virginia Woolf has been in and out, we've
reinstated Conrad, we've considered putting Joyce and Faulkner

in. Certain things don't get touched, like the *Republic* and the *Nicomachean Ethics*. We're very Greek heavy," Pearson says. "We don't do very many novels."

Pearson has also taught the undergraduate core at Chicago, her alma mater. And yes, she has noticed the slippage over the years. "Their core has eroded significantly," she says. "There is some loss in not engaging the classic texts."

It's a sight I have never forgotten. OK, the slim volume of Epictetus's *Encheiridion*, or "Handbook," was *behind* the cash register at the Columbia University bookstore, alongside other required readings for "Contemporary Civilization," one of two required core courses featuring great books. But nonetheless, there it was. Not the "Sports Illustrated Swimsuit Issue" or "What to Do If Your Roommate Is Gay," but the famous pithy Handbook by the slave with the mangled leg, who wisely counseled: "Do not seek to have events happen as you want them to, but instead want them to happen as they do happen, and your life will go well."

Columbia, more so than the University of Chicago, has doggedly clung to its legendary core curriculum, consisting mainly of readings from the great Western tradition. One of the courses, Masterpieces of Western Literature and Philosophy, aka Literature Humanities, aka LitHum, descends directly from John Erskine's General Honors class. The other required, yearlong course, Classical Civilization, or CC, likewise hails from the immediate post–World War I era, a storied Golden Age in the history of the college. Most of the college's great professors, such as Mortimer Adler, Rexford Tugwell, Mark Van Doren, Clifton Fadiman, Lionel Trilling, and Jacques Barzun, taught core courses at one time in their careers. The Western core is a favorite among alumni, often the bright shining memory of their four years on Morningside Heights, the subject of endless, dreamy ruminations in alumni publications, and progenitor of much university-sanctioned purple prose:

> At the end, the image of the core as an oasis—fertile, nourishing, and welcoming—returns. . . . But this garden needs constant tending. If Columbia College is to remain true to its most noble impulses, it must cultivate these core courses—which remain a refuge from the fleeting and the trivial—not just continue them. Isn't that what a liberal education is all about?

It is, as the marketers would say, Columbia's competitive advantage, along with the wild blandishments of New York City. Columbia distinguishes itself from competitors like Penn and Princeton by saying, If you come here, we guarantee you will receive a grounding in America's shared cultural tradition. The current core also includes art and music courses, a rocks-for-jocksy "Frontiers of Science" overview, as well as a Major Cultures (read: non-Western) and foreign-language requirement. Harvard, Yale, and Princeton can't make that claim.

What is astonishing about Columbia's core offerings is how little they have changed over the years. Timothy Cross's official history of the core highlights "changes" that seem short of earth-shattering, to say the least. Herodotus and Thucydides landed in the core in 1938; the Bible, in 1940. In 1946, Marcus Aurelius out, Tacitus in. When women arrived at Columbia in 1983, so did Jane Austen, Sappho, and Virginia Woolf. The foul-mouthed François Rabelais took a hike. The choice of Shakespeare plays often varies, but we are talking about relatively small orbital corrections in one, acknowledged solar system: the Western canon of predominantly dead white males. The current syllabus would certainly pass muster with Mortimer Adler and Robert Hutchins. Machiavelli, Descartes, Hobbes, Locke, Hume, Smith, Rousseau, Kant—the gang's all here! Allan Bloom, the late, great, best-selling scold of the American academy, should be so lucky as to be a twenty-first-century Columbia undergraduate.

At Columbia, everyone teaches the core: wildly unprepared grad students, postdoctoral adjunct professors, and the hoary tenured lions and lionesses of the humanities, who are notorious for fiddling with the prescribed curriculum. In the 1970s, a professor decided to devote most of CC's spring semester to the work of Wilhelm Dilthey, a Romantic-era German hermeneuticist whose works had hardly appeared in translation. (Oddly, the professor himself didn't know German.) Likewise, CC once fired an instructor for focusing almost exclusively on the works of Hegel and Marx, to the detriment of nondialectical thinkers. Roosevelt Montas, the current head of the core curricula, told me about a recent "aberration": A senior faculty member chose to teach only Genesis and Herodotus during the fall semester of LitHum. "That required some very delicate intervention," Montas recalls.

CC has bowed to the times, some would say, although to me it looks more like a casually indifferent shrug. W.E.B. Du Bois's *The Souls of Black Folk* has made it into the core, and most Columbia undergrads now read Mary Wollstonecraft's 1792 prefeminist tract, *Vindication of the Rights of Women*. At the end of CC's second semester, the teachers can insert readings from Hannah Arendt, Frantz Fanon, Michel Foucault, Catharine MacKinnon, John Rawls, or a text of their choosing. "That was fun," according to Jonathon Kahn, now a religion professor at Vassar, who taught

CC four times. "It's hard to find contemporary stuff," Kahn says, although he had good luck with MacKinnon and James Baldwin's *The Fire Next Time*. One year he added Jonathan Lear's challenging (to me) *Happiness, Death and the Remainder of Life* to his syllabus, and it bombed: "I had high hopes for this, it just didn't work very well. Maybe it was too personal. I found that students had a lot less tolerance for obscure contemporary texts than for obscure 17th century texts, because there was nothing but obscurity back then."

Kahn liked teaching in the core. The courses are still taught seminar-style, in keeping with the Erskine formula, although with one teacher, not two, in the classroom—again, for money reasons. Columbia requires first-year core teachers to attend weekly tutorials on the books, which some instructors are reading for the first time. The college also provides a small kitty for core socializing, to finance pizza parties or other outings. "Our class saw 'Bowling for Columbine' using the money provided by the Core office," one student reported on Columbia's course review website, "and went to the [legendary, now-closed dive] West End for the last day of class. You can't beat that." Most freshmen take LitHum, which has a common final exam, and "kids spill out into the corridors the night before the exam to study," says student Rebecca Lee. "It is very much a shared experience."

A vestigial Socraticism still prevails. Whereas Mark Van Doren once began a two-hour General Honors course by asking, "What is the role of passion in *The Iliad*?" today's teacher may be more willing to provide some historical context for the readings. The perfect core course, however, still features students, not teachers, talking. "They want the students to talk more than you, though the idea is not to make the students squirm. I would tell them, 'Next week you won't remember what Kant said, forget ten years from now,'" Kahn explains. "It's about learning how to have a conversation."

> The great thing about Columbia is that the students know they're signing up to read hard texts. There is an undergraduate determination you can count on. If you assign Kant, they're going to read it. It's nice to be in an institution where the assumption is made already. Left by themselves students are not going to force themselves to read these difficult texts. They're going to be confused, and that's the point.

I told Kahn that a friend of mine, Michael Holquist, had trouble teaching Columbia's athletes, who tended to sign up for early-morning classes, to save the afternoon for trekking to the college's faraway athletic facilities. Holquist's precise words: "They were totally at sea. They couldn't locate Greece on a map, much less have any idea about who Homer was. These were people for whom these works were just not appropriate." Kahn agreed that the early-morning time slots are tough to teach, although he felt that the engineering students "were a lot harder than the athletes."

Columbia has a separate engineering school, and its undergraduates don't have to take both CC and LitHum. They can substitute a "Major Cultures" course for a portion of the Western core and need take only one semester of either MusicHum or ArtHum. "I thought it was fabulous, it was a great experience," Jon Battat, a future graduate of the School of Engineering and Applied Sciences, told me. Other engineering schools accepted Battat, but he chose Columbia in part because of the undergraduate humanities offerings. He liked Nietzsche, Du Bois, and

MacKinnon. "Surprisingly, I enjoyed Augustine," he said. Battat plans to attend graduate school in aeronautical engineering, which is not offered at Columbia. So one day you may fly in a plane designed in part by a man who thrilled to *The Geneaology of Morals* at age 18.

The core has its discontents, and they are smart and vocal. Veteran professor Holquist, the former president of the hidebound humanities guild, the Modern Language Association, and, counterintuitively, a ferocious academic dissident, derides the "sentimental fuzz" among alumni and big Columbia donors that keeps the curriculum alive: "It's motheaten. It's death. It's perceived as an obligation by the faculty, so of course you can't expect good teaching. It's a growth that perpetuates itself."

Other professors have mocked the curriculum as "intellectual tourism," complaining that it can "lead only to a smattering of knowledge, and not to a real understanding of any one author." When classicist Francisco Barrenechea taught the core, a female student blurted out, "What's the point of learning this stuff? It's just so we can sound smart at Upper East Side dinner parties." "Another girl challenged her, and it was a lively debate," Barrenechea remembers. John Erskine heard this objection all the time, and he had a pithy comeback. "Every book, he noted, had to be read for a first time," Cross recounts in his history of the core, "and there was a profound difference between a humane familiarity with great authors and an academic exploration of them."

Another knock on the core is that there is too much of it. My son Christopher attended Columbia, and one day, as I was perusing the encyclopedic core syllabus, I asked him, "Did you *read* all those books?" Christopher admitted that in LitHum, "In the second semester I hardly read any of the books. I mean we had a week to read the *Decameron*. What I really gained was the ability to skim the classics of the Western canon." Professor Montas told me that he, too, found the core quite daunting as an undergrad. "The story among freshmen was they give you a thousand pages to read each week and you do what you can with it." Now faced with running the core, he says that "the perception is that it's too big. The faculty worry that too much undergraduate time is taken away from the students' majors." Of course, if the faculty reduces the core offerings by even one chapter in *The Wealth of Nations*, Columbia will have its own Chicago-style "core wars," complete with breathy *New York Times* op-eding to a fare thee well.*

Montas loved the core. A native of the Dominican Republic, educated in the New York City public schools, he described the core as "a transformative experience for me." Now a professor of English, he says that "my identification as an intellectual is caught up in the core." While he and I were having lunch in the late fall of 2007, he reminded me that five Columbia students were waging a hunger strike, and that one of their demands concerned changes in the core curriculum. Unlike the famous Columbia strikers of 1968, who successfully targeted the CC syllabus, these students wanted to beef up the Major Cultures course, so that they could be taught in the intense seminar style of LitHum and CC. The strikers had no quarrel with Epictetus, Virgil, Locke,

---

* A few years ago, Columbia's undergraduate satirical revue, the Varsity Show, memorably lampooned the college core. In "The Sound of Muses," blind, toga-clad Homer, played by an African-American actor, visits Columbia and no one recognizes him. They think he is Ray Charles. Homer's friend Zeus offers to teach all of Columbia's LitHum sections, and breaks into the show-stopping song, "More of the Core." Sample lyrics: "Modern books are just a distraction / Give me the ancients! / Give me the action!" In the musical, Zeus takes over the core. He lengthens each class time from two to four hours, cancels all of Columbia's noncore classes, and naturally boots all the women out of the syllabus. In a spirited dance number with Plato, Aristotle, and Dante, Virginia Woolf gives Homer an earful: "You're just another man in the canon / Writing books that I don't want to read / You might be prolific / but you're soporific indeed."

Kant, and Friedrich Engels. They were quite content to leave the dead white males right in the center of the Columbia undergraduate experience.

"Odd, isn't it?" Montas mused.

Well, yes and no.

TEN

HARD
CORE

ST. JOHN'S COLLEGE

═══════════════════════════════════════

IT IS WITH CONSIDERABLE PLEASURE that I turn my attention
to St. John's College, where the core is the core is . . . the entire
curriculum. St. John's, which has two campuses teaching almost
exactly the same courses in Annapolis, Maryland, and in Santa
Fe, New Mexico, embodies that marvelous French aphorism:
They are comfortable in their own skin.

Robert Hutchins's dream of creating a four-year-long, classical college curriculum came a cropper in Chicago. Soon after he
left the campus, the program vilified by A. J. Liebling in the *New
Yorker* as "the greatest magnet for neurotic juveniles since the
Children's Crusade" was discontinued. There is only one college in
America where the Hutchins dream lives on: St. John's, home of
the croquet-playing, Greek-maxim-spouting "Johnnies."

After the University of Chicago faculty gave them the bum's
rush in 1936,* Hutchins's paladins Stringfellow Barr and Scott

---

* Chicago's History Department scathingly assessed the omnididact Barr, damning him as
an "exceptionally pleasing person" who "makes no pretense of scholarship or scholarly pro-
ductivity in the sense in which those terms are understood at the University of Chicago."

Buchanan surfaced the following year in Annapolis, where they took over a tiny, failing, picturesque college on the banks of College Creek. Here they instituted their vaunted "New Program"— all Great Books, all the time. They fervently hoped that Robert Hutchins would abandon the Chicago morass and join them. Instead, he agreed to chair the board of trustees of St. Johns's "self-governing republic of learning." A flurry of puffy publicity greeted the first class of twenty students, only eight of whom would survive the four-year-long trek from Aristotle to Einstein. Columnist Walter Lippman, then at the apogee of his influence, hailed St. John's as "the seedbed of the American renaissance."

Hutchins visited often. One of his daughters attended St. John's, as did one of Adler's sons. Adler himself lectured at Annapolis every year, and was subjected to ever-wilder pranks because he always ran an hour or more over his allotted time. The second time he visited, the students planted alarm clocks in the auditorium, which he naturally ignored. In later years, a student dressed as an ape crossed the stage to interrupt a lecture on Darwin, and the Johnnies once cut the power to the auditorium, all in a vain attempt to get Adler to shut up. "I subsequently shortened my lectures to an hour and a half," Adler admitted.

Buchanan, a fiery teacher brandishing degrees from Amherst, Oxford, and Harvard, once said that the St. John's mission was "preparing people to be misfits" in the universe. He was a bit of a misfit himself. A Rhodes scholar who hoped to make a career in Sanskrit, he ended up studying philosophy at Harvard, which nearly rejected his doctoral dissertation. The only person said to have understood his thesis was Alfred North Whitehead, one of the world's most eminent thinkers, who informed his Harvard colleagues, "If you cannot understand this, so much the worse for you."

When Buchanan and Barr arrived at St. John's, they realized that one of them would have to become president. "Well, that would have to be you," Buchanan told his friend, "because I don't answer my mail." Buchanan turned aside a badly needed grant from the Rockefeller Foundation because he felt its "conventional system of grading and calculating degree credits would confuse and distort the sharp critical judgments that we would need to make in maintaining our course and correcting our mistakes." At St. John's, students see their grades only by request. Some teachers still object to assigning grades, which is done to help students who are transferring to other colleges or applying to graduate school. The main evaluative tool is the "don rag," a twice-yearly meeting between a student and his or her assembled teachers.

Like Buchanan, President Barr was a free spirit. St. John's staffer Rosemary Harty directed me to Barr's 95-page essay on "Growing Vegetables" that kicks off *The Kitchen Garden Cookbook*. "If I have been guilty [of 'garrulity']," Barr writes on page 94, "I ask pardon—but there was so much to talk about." That's St. John's in a nutshell; the talk never stops. The college's famous, two-hour-long evening seminars often repair to the coffee shop afterward, and then spill into the dormitory corridors. "We talk about our souls," sophomore Clint Richardson told me amidst the clattering of the college's only dining hall, adding, "I like truth a lot. I really value truth." In our conversation, Richardson, a graduate of Michigan's East Lansing High School, used the adverb *eidetically* in the presence of three classmates. It was obvious that I was the only person at the table who would be heading for the dictionary, to learn that *eidetically* means something like "visually." Welcome to the republic of learning.

In seventy years, practically nothing has changed at the postage stamp–sized college in Annapolis, a historic landmark now hemmed in by the U.S. Naval Academy on one side and a surprisingly tasteful public housing development on the other. All teachers, regardless of previous academic standing, are called tutors. Tutors address the students as "Mr. Smith" and "Ms. Jones" in class. All tutors must eventually learn to teach every course, so Nick Maistrellis, who did five years of graduate work in the history of science, had to learn how to teach Greek and French, the college's two required languages. Tenure is awarded for teaching only. A tenured tutor, Susan Paalman, received her PhD in biophysics from Johns Hopkins and taught middle school before coming to Annapolis. In high school, college, and graduate school, she had never read *The Iliad*, *The Odyssey*, nor Plato. Now she teaches them. "From a practical point of view, there are drawbacks," says Santa Fe tutor Emily Rena-Dozier, who teaches Euclid but hasn't studied geometry since high school. "Because we teach every course, we are incompetent in a number of fields. We really aim to be the best naive readers imaginable." There is a hoary joke about how having a PhD "is no barrier to being hired at St. John's, but it can't help."

You can see the entire four years' curriculum on the Internet. All students take two years of ancient Greek, two years of French, four years of math, and three years of laboratory science. Yes, Great Books science. The freshmen read Lavoisier's *Elements of Chemistry*, and the seniors read Faraday and Heisenberg.* Johnnies

---

* After he left the college in 1946, Buchanan started inveighing against the New Program. When he returned to speak at Commencement the following year, he was beating the drum for a "permanent revolutionary committee" that would continually overhaul the curriculum. Heretically, he urged the inclusion of non-Western literature in the program: "We ought to have gone at the Oriental books simply and hard, and we'd have cracked them," he said. "The best way to learn these things is to teach them. . . . Don't stand on your competence."

score well on the law boards and the graduate school exams. If a boy or girl wants to attend medical school, that means an additional year or year and a half of memorizing facts in conventional Biology and Chemistry classes, not learning the "truth" behind the science, Great Books–style. "Facts are the core of an anti-intellectual curriculum," Robert Hutchins thundered in 1933. But they come in handy if you want to pass the MCAT.

The curriculum hardly ever changes. Yes, Justinian was dropped from the syllabus, but tutor and former dean Eva Brann, who has taught at St. John's for fifty years, can't remember exactly when. A tutor who has taught there for ten years could name only one curriculum change: Aeschylus's *Prometheus Bound* was deleted from the freshman reading list and replaced by Aristophanes's *The Birds*. Naturally, the school tries to capitalize on its musty offerings. "The following teachers will return to St. John's next year: Beethoven, Euclid, Plato, Toqueville . . ." is the text of a successful promotional campaign that has been printed up on postcards and mailed to high schoolers taking Advanced Placement exams. Very often, it is the first contact prospective students have with the college, which, even after seventy years, is not very well known, and is considered an oddity in traditional academic circles.

I first saw Brann speak in 2006 at a Great Books conference at Yale, where she shared a stage with former University of Chicago president Hanna Gray, Yale's president Richard Levin, and Harvey Mansfield, a high-profile, conservative professor of government at Harvard. Brann, short, cheerful, gnomic, and embarking on her ninth decade, is probably the best-known ambassador for St. John's in the outside world. A Yale-trained archaeologist, she won a National Humanities Medal in 2005 and exudes enthusiasm for the college's distinctive program. St. John's created a handsome, bound version of a long essay by Brann as the centerpiece for a recent capital campaign, and some of her pronouncements doubtless welled up many an alumni eye. "Why ancient Greek, a dead language?" Brann asks in her essay, and then answers her own question, Johnnie-style: "Well, it isn't dead to us and it's beautiful." She rejects the notion that St. John's is backward-looking: "No school was ever less interested in bygones than ours." Rena-Dozier told me that some of her most exciting classes were devoted to the first-century astronomer Ptolemy. "We spent several months in freshman and sophomore math figuring out the equations that explain how the sun revolves around the earth, which I've been told it doesn't," she said. "It turns out to be quite a fascinating discussion, why we think the facts we think are facts are facts, and why do we care? Students get really het up about Ptolemy. There is something to be said for non-utilitarian learning."

At the Yale conference, Mansfield mocked Harvard's latest remix of its undergraduate core, which he said demonstrated "a hostility to great books that was not previously present in the curriculum." Revamping curricula was not a subject that Brann could warm to. "We don't think particular times require particular educations," Brann said on the podium. "St. John's College is not for the next thing. It's for its own sake." Gray, a Renaissance historian, gently chided Brann and St. John's for offering no history courses in its curriculum. History, you will remember, is mere facts, not knowledge. "We do teach history," Brann countered, with a hint of defensiveness in her voice. "Thucydides . . . Tacitus. Unfortunately, it stops there."

When I approached Brann about visiting St. John's, she reacted enthusiastically. "Send a letter to the dean, and send me a copy, too," she said, adding, "A real letter, of course, not something electronic."

So what is St. John's like? First off, it's beautiful. The thirty-six-acre campus is dotted with eighteenth-century colonial buildings and houses, and rises from the low-lying athletic fields next to College Creek up to McDowell Hall, a stately, three-story neo-Palladian classroom building originally built as a residence for the governor of Maryland. Annapolis remains Maryland's capital, and the city center has become an opulent boutique village, like Georgetown or Alexandria in the nearby Washington, D.C., area. Even if it had a huge endowment, which it doesn't, St. John's could never grow, bound as it is by the Creek, the village, the Academy, and the housing development. The surrounding real estate is so expensive that few tutors can afford to live in the vicinity.

What is it like, apart from eidetically? "It's weird," commented one prominent conservative educator, who is lionized when he visits Annapolis but preferred to keep his reservations private. I suppose it is a bit weird that college club presidents and team captains are called *archons*—Greek for "leader"—and the student body is referred to as the Polity. One of the girls' intramural sports team is called the Kunai, Greek for "hell bitches." Weird, yes. But weird in a good way.

It's interesting that Buchanan would claim to be churning out "misfits" at his new college, as most students apply to St. John's because they are already misfits. As a prank, some St. John's seniors posted an amusing "promotional video" for the college on YouTube. It starts off with two bedraggled, cigarette-puffing stoners driving through the countryside, while one sings the virtues of this college where "things are a little different." "They call the teachers 'tutors,' they call the textbooks 'manuals,' and you know what they call the essence of the thing? 'Ousia.'" That line would have them rolling in the aisles in Annapolis and Santa Fe, where the lowliest freshman encounters the present participle of

A classically proportioned Trojan Horse, placed by the Johnnies against the wall of the U.S. Naval Academy, "School that's based on sin."

the Greek verb *to be*, which also means "essence," moments after arriving on campus.

The boys and girls who end up on the banks of College Creek tend to be kids who just can't get with the program. And who can possibly defend the program? Practically all high school courses are now taught to one test or another, whether it be a state-mandated "high-stakes" graduation test or one of the ever-expanding galaxy of Advanced Placement exams considered *de rigueur* for entry to a top-tier college. Even the calmest of parents succumb to anxiety during the college application nightmare, and children detect the disturbance in the spheres, whether they surrender to it or not. Learning takes a backseat to succeeding—

succeeding on the standardized tests, succeeding at sports, and suc-ceeding at extracurricular activities. What's to like? The system breeds dissidents. Many of them drop out. Some apply to St. John's.

Traditionally, the college has been happy to have them. They call them "risks," kids with checkered (read: bad) high school transcripts who write convincing essays about why they want to read the Great Books at St. John's. (Until recently, the University of Chicago tried to drink from this same applicant pool, with its wildly nonstandard [e.g., "Tell us about mustard"] "Uncommon App," or college application.) All incoming freshmen are a risk, because no boy or girl among them has ever sat at a seminar table in a school where they who teach best teach least, and whose motto is "a full notebook betokens an empty mind." A by-product of increased college applications has been an attenuated sense of daring on the part of St. John's, because it can be more choosy. "In the past, we took a fair number of risks," says Dean Michael Dink. "We now ask, 'Are we eager to take this risk?' versus, 'Are we willing to take this risk?'"

Unlike almost every other college in America, St. John's has a high freshman washout rate. Of an entering class of 140, only 100 used to graduate. Now probably 110 or 115 will. Also unlike most colleges, it has a 60-40 male-to-female ratio. The names on the syllabus are practically all male, which turns off some female ap-plicants. St. John's is pretty easy to get into—the college accepts about 60 percent of the self-selecting high school seniors who apply—but tough to stay in.

Kids drop out because studying the Great Books is hard. I at-tended several classes during my visit, all of which surprised me. A senior laboratory devoted to Ernest Rutherford's essay "The Scattering of Alpha and Beta Particles by Matter and the Structure of the Atom" was flat, flat, flat. No one seemed to have done the reading, and if anyone had, not much was taken in. A sophomore Greek class treated me to their morning pledge. Rising from their seats in ancient McDowell Hall (Lafayette ate here!), the boys and girls faced east and chanted, "For I am Oedipus, whom all men call great." In Greek, of course. The liveliest class of all was a sophomore mathematics discussion of the *Conics* of Appollonius of Perga, a book so stultifying that Adler purged it from the 1990 Great Books. "This is actually really interesting," one student blurted out as he monkeyed around at the blackboard. "It shows how the parabola is straightening out." Speaking about Appollonius, student Molly Rothenberg told me, "Our tutor said that no one else in the world is studying this guy. And it is really, really hard."

"These kids do not remind me of myself," I wrote in my notebook during my sojourn in the St. John's classrooms. I meant it as a compliment.

Brann allowed me to sit in on her sophomore seminar that evening, devoted to Questions 2–5 of Aquinas's *Summa Theologica*. At St. John's, the two-hour evening seminar is the Main Event. Twenty-five minutes before the 8 P.M. start, I felt the campus buzzing; every student was hurrying with apparent enthusiasm to his or her classroom. "Our Great Books seminars are in the evening when the young tend to be loquacious," Brann explained, also advising me ahead of time that the assigned reading was "stupefying." I would have to agree. The two hours devoted to Aquinas's famous treatise on God did not go well at all. Like myself, everyone had done the reading, but few could make heads or tails of it. Brann herself floated the most interesting idea of the evening, that perhaps Aquinas was making God absolutely impossible to love—"an intense, white light" is how one student phrased it—to emphasize the role of Jesus Christ as our necessary mediator with the Divine. Anything is possible.*

You live by the Books, and you die by the Books. This is the downside of the "Great Books will do the teaching" pedagogy. Suppose the books fail in their mission? I thought of a thousand interesting questions to ask about Aquinas: Why did he feel the necessity of proving God's existence? Who in the Middle Ages disagreed with him? What was the purpose of the twenty-two volumes of the *Summa Theologica*? Why was he so fat that he had difficulty walking across a room? "We don't talk that much about who the actual people are," Rothenberg complained to me. Like St. Augustine, for instance. On her own, she found out that "he persecuted and tortured the heretics. Sometimes we're missing the historical context."

If you teach the Great Books by the Erskine-Hutchins-Adler book, as they still do at St. John's and in the few remaining Great Books seminars around the country, all those questions are out of order. Only the text on the table is allowed to speak. But that's a mistake. There is plenty to learn from outside the book, and I daresay a professor with a PhD in theology could have brought much to our meager table that night. In education, as in all pursuits, extreme solutions always bear the seeds of their own failure. Even Aristotle knew that. You can look it up.

To say that student life at St. John's is distinctive would be a wild understatement. To be sure, the boys and girls at Annapolis look

---

* G. K. Chesterton writes of a lady friend who picked up a selection from Aquinas titled *The Simplicity of God*. She faltered, put down the book, and said, "Well, if that's His simplicity, I wonder what His complexity is like."

like normal college kids, dressing slovenly, spending their days shambling from one gorgeous eighteenth-century neo-Classical classroom building to another. I thought I saw more smokers on campus than usual, which would fit with my Johnnies-as-social-dissenters theory. But that is far from the only deviation from the college norm. At a typical college, for instance, friends on the ubiquitous Facebook.com might rally around a sports team, or a favorite watering hole. Here are the names of two typical St. John's Facebook groups: "I didn't get laid because I was too busy reading Thucydides" and "I had to look up 'logos.'"

Take sports. St. John's offers only three sports: sailing, crew, and fencing, with a heavy emphasis on intramural competition. The men's teams have names like the Guardians and the Spartans; the women are the Maenads, Amazons, Furies, Nymphs, and Kunai. Recent graduate John Okrent remembers rowing against a small school in Maryland when "suddenly our cox started screaming to us about the soul, doing this little Aristotle bit to inspire us. It was kind of annoying, actually." It is true that the Johnnies are never shy about flashing their erudition. When some students were arrested during a civil rights demonstration in the early 1960s, the *Saturday Review* quoted a student who observed: "Annapolis has the only jail cell in the country with Greek inscriptions on the cell walls."

Athletic director Leo Pickens is a former student, a trim, thoughtful Californian who grew up in a home that owned Britannica's Great Books of the Western World. "Their iconic presence was huge," he recalled, balancing on a thick plastic yoga ball in St. John's dowdy gym. "You're right, though, they were impossible to read. Those two columns of dense type. It was very off-putting." He had fond memories of Robert Hutchins's introductory essay, "The Great Conversation." Within moments,

Pickens and I were discussing arête, the Greek concept of virtue that also includes attributes of knowledge and heroism. "Excellence is a daily habit of some virtue," Pickens explained. "I'm trying to get the students to prize arête, the Greek quality of virtue and excellence." Like *eidetically*, this is a word I am hearing for the first time. It is omnipresent in the work of Homer, Plato, and Aristotle, and is of course familiar to every St. John's freshman.

How come, I asked Pickens, the Johnnies are so ferociously competitive? At a spring festival called "Reality," intended to usher the seniors out of the Platonic cave where they have dwelt for four years, the students play "Spartan Madball," a semicontrolled riot staged on the flat plain of the lower campus with a huge, inflated bladder. The game ends "only when three goals have been made or three ambulances have been called." Off the playing fields, it is said, the classically educated Johnnies party harder than anyone north of Florida State.

"That is a good question," Pickens said. "Look, the students want to be here. They want to learn. They want to read these books. That bleeds over into all these extracurriculars. They have that splendid intensity that you so rarely find in America anymore."

That intensity flares up every spring for The Game, a quarter-century-old rivalry between St. John's and the Naval Academy in . . . croquet. Long dominated by the Johnnies, the resurgent midshipmen recently hired a coach and bought fancy new mallets. But the *Washington Post*, among others, has suggested that the middies may never match the Great Bookies in the splendid intensity department. St. John's "brings a three-pronged attack passed down from one imperial wicket [team captain] to the next," the newspaper reported in 2006. "Practice hard, play all out, drink heavily and find new and creative ways to put the

War by other means: the famous St. John's–Naval Academy croquet match.
COURTESY OF ST. JOHN'S COLLEGE

minds off their game." In what might be a nod to Aristophanes, the *Post* reported, "The Johnnies also field a Designated Temptress, held in reserve for desperate moments, whose job it is to saunter over to the midshipmen with a winning smile and a tray of drinks."

In 1987, the St. John's fans broke into this derisive chant:

Naval Academy, School of War,
School that's based on sin.
St. John's College, School of Knowledge,
We are going to win.

Arête? Or hubris? The gods spoke; St. John's lost.

"The Johnnies take this sport very seriously," Pickens confirmed. "They love nothing more than to chop up on the middies. They play a very aggressive form of croquet."

They also play an aggressive form of kicking back. "They seem to party with a vengeance," Okrent told me. "It's like they're out to prove something. Maybe it's from reading about all those heroic men." Wednesday night—*Wednesday* night—is known as "New Year's Eve" at hard-partying Annapolis, and the administration has occasionally imposed curfews on student revels.

Okrent, who plans to attend medical school, is experiencing one of the downsides of St. John's. He needs to be reeducated to even apply to become a doctor. And there is another downside. Taking postgraduate pre-med courses at Bennington College, he said, "is very jarring." "At St. John's, there was a productive sort of wonder in the wandering in the classroom. Your mind isn't used to processing information just to get the answer. Now the dialectic is gone. The teachers are just teaching, the students just sit there listening. We're just learning to get a good grade on the test."

The biggest problem St. John's students described to me was withdrawal, and interactions with a world that doesn't give a fig about the Great Books. Even during the blotto, midweek "New Year's Eves," Okrent said, the students kept talking about the pursuit of knowledge; "I haven't had those conversations since I left St. John's." "It's almost impossible to explain to friends what we're doing here," student Paul Wilford said. "It looks like we're just taking a bunch of introductory courses."

Molly Rothenberg lives not too far from me in the Boston area, and I shared a hamburger with her during one of her Christmas breaks. She told me about sitting down with a fellow graduate of the Cambridge (Massachusetts) Rindge and Latin School during sophomore year. Her friend was attending Bates College in Maine. "She told me they were studying Rhetoric, and they would be watching episodes of 'Desperate Housewives' and listening to Eminem. They were going to analyze it. I just laughed. What could I say?"

ELEVEN

AMONG
THE BOOKIES

===============

THE GREAT BOOKS ARE NOT IN FASHION. Harold and Allan Bloom notwithstanding, the literary canon has broadened to encompass slave narratives and the utterances of Chief Joseph Seattle, among others. For its fiftieth anniversary collection of twentieth-century writings published in 1997, the Great Books Foundation included an excerpt from Vladimir Nabokov's *Lolita*, which elicited predictable howls of protest. Today, in their Great Conversations collections of poems and short stories, they publish snippets of Dave Eggers, Sogyal Rimpoche, and Maya Angelou. "You want to operate in the spirit of Adler, but not in the letter," Foundation staffer Dan Born explained to me. "Some people say we're departing from the pure faith of Mortimer Adler, but great literature continues be written. You can't talk about Aristotle forever. We don't want to be stuck in a deep freeze."

Against all odds, the Great Books movement is not dead. It is true that there are no more Great Books salesmen knocking on doors, masquerading as university professors, and subjecting their marks to the "Mexican build-up" and other dubious sales practices. In fact, there are hardly any more Great Books sales. Britannica, which Benton's heirs unloaded on Lebanese-Canadian investor Jacqui Safra, makes no attempt to sell off the inventory left over from the disastrous 1990 relaunch. If you happen to trip across them on the company's website, you can buy the set for $1,200. "We don't market them aggressively," admits Britannica's Tom Panelas. "There isn't a groundswell of demand for the books."

The Great Books Foundation, created in 1947 to service the viral outbreak of postwar reading groups, still claims 850 active chapters, although hardly any of them actually read the Hutchins-Adler-Benton selections. The Foundation has been on the verge of bankruptcy more than once, most recently in 2002, when it laid off a quarter of its staff. President George Schueppert, a straight-talking businessman with a background in engineering and corporate finance, waxes unsentimental about the halcyon days of the Western canon. "The organization had an inspiring mission but no business plan," he says. "It was clear that the founders' idea that there was a vast craving for liberal arts education that would lead to tens of thousands of participants and hundreds of thousands of book sales—that never happened."

A lot of what could have gone wrong, has gone wrong. About ten years into its existence, Schueppert relates, the Foundation gave up on the idea of making money from the adult reading groups. "We've never been able to do what Hutchins and Adler thought was possible," he explains, "to get adults to pay for the books and for training of the leaders. Sputnik was our saving grace"—for a while, at least. Panicked by the Soviet Union's 1957 launch of the beachball-sized, chirping satellite, America poured money into "gifted and talented" courseware for the nation's elementary schools, and the Great Books were more than welcome. But those programs have now largely vanished, decimated first by anti-elitist groupthink and then, more definitively, by the George

W. Bush administration's No Child Left Behind program, which emphasizes "teaching to the test." Startlingly, the Foundation has failed to cash in on the lucrative book club phenomenon, because it holds itself above it. Schueppert speaks dismissively about Oprah's Winfrey's book club and the thousands of reading klatches that it has spawned. "We'll read *To Kill a Mockingbird*, but we're not going to ask, 'How do you feel about the lead character?' The Great Books movement isn't about feelings, it is about interpretation. We are hosting an intellectual event, not a social event."

And so an opportunity passes.

While writing this book, I attended two Great Books Weekends, Friday-evening-through-Sunday-lunch events, with each day devoted to one of three books. The current M.O. seems to be this: one piece of classical literature, such as *Gilgamesh* and *Oedipus Rex*; some modern literature, such as Sherwood Anderson's *Winesburg, Ohio* or *The Hummingbird's Daughter* by Luis Albert Urrea. Then something from in between. At a weekend in Chicago, it was Jonathan Swift's "Voyage to the Houyhnhnms" from *Gulliver's Travels*. At a late winter confab in Mystic, Connecticut, we read "The Future of an Illusion," Sigmund Freud's brief, corrosive, and semiconvincing essay about the eventual withering away of religion. In each case, these are books I would never have re-read, or read at all. Reading them *en groupe* turned out to be fun, and also hard.

How does it work? You send the Foundation a check for a few hundred dollars, and they send you the three books that will be discussed, months ahead of time. There goes your excuse for not getting to the material. The latter-day Great Bookies gather on a Friday afternoon at a not-so-bad businessperson's hotel and see which discussion group they have landed in. When I showed up at the Mystic Hilton for the New England Great Books Council's weekend—organized around the theme "Would You Believe. . . ?"—I found myself one of fourteen members of "The Enkidoodle Dandies," a reference to Gilgamesh's boon companion and object of homoerotic affection, Enkidu. Other groups were "The Freudy Cats," "The Ishtar Gazers," and so on. Corny? Yes.

How to put this? I myself am of a certain age, but it seemed as if practically everyone else attending the meeting was older. I felt younger than most of the people there, many of whom were retirees, and many of whom seemed to have been schoolteachers. Women outnumbered men by about two to one. Almost everyone had attended Great Books events before, and there seemed to be some artful politicking going on, as the veterans angled to be assigned to a "good" group, like college kids angling for the cool T.A. Peter Temes, Schueppert's predecessor at the Great Books Foundation, also noticed the graying—nay, whitening—of his core audience. "I went out and saw some of these groups," he says. "It was scary. I don't think that's reversible. It's suitable for a generation that's on its last legs."

On Friday evening, we gathered for a warm-up discussion of two poems that we hadn't read before coming: Elizabeth Bishop's "Sestina" and "Choose Something Like a Star" by Robert Frost. Whatever I spent, my money came back to me in those two hours. I have a "thing" about Bishop. Could they have known? I once drove my family hundreds of miles off the beaten track just to see the house where she grew up in Great Village, Nova Scotia. The Frost poem sounded hauntingly familiar. In the ten minutes at the end of the class reserved for introducing materials from "outside" the book, a woman from Cambridge, Massachusetts, and I both realized that we had heard the same performance of the Randall Thompson choral version of "Star" at a tiny morning chapel service on the Harvard campus. It was, literally, unforgettable.

How was the intellectual experience? In the case of these two poems—fantastic. I hadn't participated in a classroom discussion in at least thirty years, and this particular brand of poetry—careful, revealing, intelligent but not abstruse—lends itself perfectly to filling up an evening with cheerfully exchanged discoveries. I would call both poems beautiful, and hard, but not impossible to understand and to love. And we literate citizens around the table, like sparrows with tiny crumbs in our beaks, each brought a little meaning, or experience, or knowledge, to each carefully crafted line. My first Great Books experience turned out to be one of my best.

On Saturday we discussed Freud in the morning and then Stephen Mitchell's jaunty, sexy, and partly fictional rendition of *Gilgamesh* in the afternoon. I say fictional because there are large gaps in the 4,000-year-old epic, which Mitchell fills in masterfully. Here is the animal-like Enkidu's first encounter with the fruits of civilization:

> She [the priestess Shamhat] stripped off her robe and lay there naked, with her legs apart, touching herself. Enkidu saw her and warily approached. He sniffed the air. He gazed at her body. He drew close, Shamhat touched him on the thigh, touched his penis, and put him inside her. She used her love-arts, she took his breath with her kisses, held nothing back, and showed him what a woman is.

That's what I call a great book!

The old John Erskine rules governing "shared inquiry," the ones still scrupulously observed at St. John's, were in effect. We received a printed sheet of discussion guidelines, which almost everyone but me already knew by heart: "Read the entire book more than once." (I didn't.) "Discuss only the book everyone has read." (I did.) "Speak Up, Join In . . . Back Up Your Statements, Listen Carefully . . . Be Courteous," and so on.

But the inflexible rules seem silly, especially when we have excellent textual notes to Stephen Mitchell's jazzy new translation of *Gilgamesh* right inside the book itself. Likewise, Peter Gay's brief introduction to our slender Freud essay contains the tantalizing biographical detail that Freud, after suffering for years from a painful jaw cancer, asked his friend and doctor, Max Schur, to kill him with a lethal injection of morphine. Surely this was a man who was not a slave to religious illusions of the kind he describes in his famous essay.

The last ten minutes of each two-hour session are a free-for-all, and anyone can introduce facts and stories from outside the book. Sometimes these tiny aperçus are the most revealing moments of all. In *Hummingbird*, the very long Urrea novel, the author notes that the protagonist, his relative Teresita, who was credited with shamanistic healing powers in her native Mexico, eventually found her way to New York City. One of our classmates learned that she became a model for the turn-of-the-nineteenth-century ideal of feminine beauty, the Gibson Girl.

My group was funny. One woman seemed on the edge of a nervous collapse. A woman dressed in a track suit with extravagantly disheveled "red" hair proved to be brilliant, and then mysteriously developed laryngitis after our first meeting and was never seen again. A too-serious-for-my-tastes retiree, who was extremely well prepared for Freud and for the Sumerian epic, refused to participate in our discussion of *The Hummingbird's Daughter*. He sent word through an intermediary that he thought the novel was too frivolous to merit serious discussion. Mortimer Adler would agree, but I don't.

The curse of every Great Books group is someone like Henry the hydrologist—not his real name or profession—who knows a little and talks a lot. It's people like him that the veterans know to avoid. His wife seemed smart, but she was not in our group. Husbands and wives are never paired in these seminars. If his wife had been there, she would have told him to clam up, and that would have been the end of it. Henry regaled us with his understanding of fluid dynamics, and initiated exchanges like this one:

HENRY: "Man is basically good, we're a herding animal."

WOMAN ON HENRY'S RIGHT, ROLLING HER EYEBALLS, FOR THE NTH TIME: "But that's not what Freud is saying."

HENRY: "Yes, but that's what I am saying."

Saturday night's suggested activity was "an evening of informal board and card games and a chance to socialize." I had already been socializing, after the Great Books fashion. In the bar, and at mealtimes, the common conversational icebreaker was: "How was your Freud?" or "How was your *Gilgamesh*?" The answers vary, depending on which group your interlocutor landed in. "Very lively"; "Pretty good"; or "It never really came together." This must be what it's like to attend St. John's College, every day of the year.

So I passed on socializing and repaired to my room to watch some of the "March Madness" NCAA semifinal basketball games on television, which were particularly dramatic that year. My roommate was a genial, 80-something retired schoolteacher from upstate New York. For each book discussion, he had prepared a sheaf of notes, written out in a narrow, precise hand. He stared at the basketball game on the oversized screen, eyeing each flash-and-dash Gatorade or deodorant commercial as if seeing TV for the first time. "I don't get to a lot of television," he remarked quietly, emphasizing the obvious.

I had other Great Books experiences, most of them equally memorable. For its annual Great Books weekend in its hometown of Chicago, the Great Books Foundation organizes a cultural wingding. In 2007, to celebrate the theme "Know Thyself," the Foundation sponsored a screening of Julie Taymor's disturbing, Japanese film version of *Oedipus Rex* and a matinee at the Alvin Ailey dance theater. But the books were the real stars. I fell off my seat laughing at the *Houyhnhnms*—every author can relate to a narrator who gets crapped on by screaming ninnies in trees—although my fellow Bookies engaged Swift with a grim, determined seriousness. "This is *funny stuff*!" I exclaimed to a roomful of readers, as I watched Swift's best material die like a decaffeinated Vegas lounge act. There was no reaction. Everyone wanted to talk about identity and the self.

The people of the Books are earnest to a fault, which is not to say that I didn't learn from them. While revisiting *Winesburg, Ohio*, one woman kept insisting that George Willard, the book's narrator, was impotent. There's plenty of evidence that he's not. For instance, Willard fires up a cigar right after an encounter with the town floozie. But I can see that sex scares him quite a bit. I hadn't thought of that.

A 2008 Great Books discussion group in Chicago.
COPYRIGHT © 2008 BY THE GREAT BOOKS FOUNDATION

I also started visiting my local public library, which had been hosting monthly Great Books sessions more or less forever. We have read portions of Richard Tawney's fascinating *Religion and the Rise of Capitalism*, certainly not a book one would have come across, nor I daresay a book that is taught much anymore. The library groups are free and open to anyone, and a predictable barn dance ensues. Tawney wrote a compelling intellectual and social history of seventeenth-century England, but my Newton, Massachusetts, neighbors wanted to talk about Mormonism, the presidential elections, the state of Indiana, almost anything that came to mind. One night, while we were discussing Edward Gibbon's *The Rise and Fall of the Roman Empire*, a participant remarked that Gibbon was considered to be the worst writer, ever, in the English language. I had heard considerable sniping at Gibbon's serpentine prose style over the years, but "worst ever" seemed a bit strong. It turned out that the reader had confused Gibbon with Edward Bulwer-Lytton, of "A dark and stormy night . . ." fame, who has lent his name to an annual contest of bad writing. Oh, well. Never mind. At a subsequent session, we read Machiavelli's *The Prince*, which occasioned much George W. Bush–bashing, for whatever reasons. "Sort of like an Albee play," my notes read. "Sharp intellects and lost souls."

Reading *The Prince*, we encountered the same problem that prompted William Benton to publish the Great Books of the Western World in the first place. We all had different translations and editions, and couldn't follow one another's textual allusions. I own the Benton-Britannica *Prince*, but because the double-column narrow type is unreadable, I used a Harvey Mansfield translation I bought at the University of Chicago bookstore. This in no way alleviated the textual nightmare. A good half-hour was wasted discussing whether Machiavelli ever said "the ends justify the means," which is certainly suggested by some of the English renderings. But how would we know? And the ten different translations represented at the table didn't help at all.

If the Great Books were a stock, would you invest in them? Looking around the room at the white-haired shareholders, you would have to say no. But Great Books Foundation president Schueppert remains loyal to the product. "We're going to keep the brand name," he told me in his modest office in Chicago's Jewelry Building. "We are going to champion the notion of shared inquiry. We do have a door opener in the name, and it's sad that we have never been able to capitalize on a brand that so many people praise. It's seen as a high-quality brand that regular people could never engage in. When we propose the books for use in school systems they think, 'Oh, those are the books by old guys with robes and beards.'"

TWELVE

DEAD BOOKS
WALKING

===

S O WHO KILLED THE GREAT BOOKS? Certain persons have to
be held harmless, among them Aeschylus, Dostoyevsky, and
William Shakespeare. The assassination of the Great Books is
like the famous plot of Agatha Christie's *Murder on the Orient
Express*; everyone was guilty. Hutchins, Adler, and Benton signed
a pact with the devil of commerce, and hawked their books the
way Benton sold his Crest toothpaste. Forget that it cleans your
teeth; you'll be popular! Wisdom of the ages, schmisdom of the
ages. Forget about learning—your boss will be impressed, women
will seek you out ("Oh! You're reading Fourier's 'Theory of Heat.'
. . . How fascinating!"), your kids will get into college, and so
on. The frenzy of overselling provoked a predictable reaction from
the tastemakers of the Eastern elite who had mistrusted
Hutchins's and Adler's ambitious plans for general education
from the get-go. Soon enough the Great Books were synonymous
with boosterism, Babbittry, and H. L. Mencken's benighted
boobocracy. They were everything that was wrong, unchic, and
middlebrow about middle America.

Television, too, drove a stake through the heart of the American living room, shattering what Allan Bloom called "the real

American privacy." Faux-leather-bound, double-column text-books were no match for the nonstop thrills and gags of the flittering little blue-gray screen. The half-century-long attack on the American attention span began sometime after 1950, social historian Joan Shelley Rubin wrote: "The rise of television heightened Americans' preoccupation with celebrity and further devalued the idea that acquiring knowledge required patient, disciplined training." In short order the Great Books became the "colorful furniture" that the acerbic Hutchins feared they might. He had always had his doubts. "A classic," he liked to say, "is by definition a book no one reads."

The culture wars of the 1980s effectively buried the Great Books in a blizzard of anti-Establishment, multicultural rhetoric. The academy turned against the dead white males whose busts adorned the friezes atop university libraries, and the defenders of the classical tradition—the best-selling Chicago philosopher Bloom and the octogenarian Adler—did themselves few favors in the struggle for the American mind. Bloom claimed the classics on behalf of intellectual conservatives, and planted the flag of right-wing politics smack in the middle of Hutchins's sixty-two-inch-wide shelf. This was more than ironic, as Hutchins, the one-worlder who dreamed about framing a world constitution, was a frequent target of the House Un-American Activities Committee. The animating idea behind publishing the Great Books, aside from making money for Britannica and for the University of Chicago, was populism, not elitism. Hutchins and Adler "sought the redistribution of cultural capital," according to historian Tim Lacy, who went on to observe that it all ended badly. The Great Books, he writes, "became a despised cultural commodity."

Now the fingerprints of conservative politics are all over the Great Books, with shadowy connections made between the volumes and Allan Bloom's mentor, the purported "father of neocon-servativism," Leo Strauss, who taught at Chicago and St. John's. ("Hired at the University of Chicago on the basis of a single interview with Robert Maynard Hutchins, who shared his passion for the classics," Jacob Heilbrunn writes in *They Knew They Were Right: The Rise of the Neocons*, Strauss "wanted his students to return to the great books.") Signals get confused in translation. Strauss and Bloom were both intellectual conservatives, but also confirmed elitists. Where cultural capital was concerned they were hoarders, not sharers.

Conspiracy types like to point out that Joyce Rumsfeld, wife of the former secretary of defense, sat on the board of directors at St. John's, Santa Fe, and that the two St. John's have received (modest) grants from the right-wing Olin and Bradley Foundations. (Harvard and Yale have, too.) These nefarious associations supposedly explain the George W. Bush administration's decision to send a former president of St. John's, John Agresto, to reestablish Iraq's Ministry of Education after the 2003 invasion. In retrospect, it was a fool's errand. Alas, they picked the wrong fool. Agresto wrote a harsh, articulate indictment of Bush's Iraq reconstruction policies, *Mugged by Reality: The Liberation of Iraq and the Failure of Good Intentions*.

Right-wingers do love the great books. The conservative Manhattan Institute has created a Veritas Fund to support classical curricula. The conservative Liberty Fund, headquartered in Indianapolis, publishes many Great Books texts "to encourage study of the ideal of a society of free and responsible individuals." The rightward gravitational pull is real enough so that Clare Pearson, who runs that vestigial Great Books program for the University of Chicago's extension school, no longer promotes her connection to the famous brand. "We try to distance ourselves from it a bit," she told me. "Unfortunately, a lot of the Great Books movement has become associated with the political right. These books don't put forth any univocal political view that we can discern, so the label isn't very useful anymore."

Another problem: Many men and women who love the Great Books love them too well. Great Books Foundation president George Schueppert is correct to worry that his brand conjures up images "of old guys with robes and beards," because a stultifying, high-poetic seriousness has sapped much strength from the enterprise. The two Britannica sets are almost unreadable, with potentially awe-inspiring works of art mummified in cheapo-depot, public-domain translations. To have them on one's shelf, as I do, is to experience their serried, sepia-toned reproach: Why haven't you finished Plato's *Symposium*? they ask. Lord knows I tried, but I had no idea who half the characters were, and furthermore, why is Alcibiades hitting on Socrates? Dear Mr. Hutchins: Enquiring minds require explanatory introductions, and footnotes.

Somehow, somewhere, someone drained the energy and fun out of the Great Books. It was depressing for me to sit through the aforementioned doleful wake of *Gulliver's Travels*. Hutchins obviously anticipated the no-fun problem by begging for the inclusion of *Tristram Shandy* in the Great Books of the Western World, because he hoped it would lighten the load. More Mark Twain, less Marcus Aurelius? It's just an idea. It was disconcerting to think that someone would boycott an assigned book, such as *The Hummingbird's Daughter*, just because it was a modern novel. In my mind's ear, I hear the raspy, hectoring voice of Mortimer Adler: All the great books were modern, once.

———

"It's hard to resist poking fun at 'The Great Books of the Western World,'" *Washington Post* book critic Michael Dirda wrote in his 2003 literary memoir, *An Open Book*. His working-class parents paid $400 for a Great Books set when he was a teenager in Ohio in the 1960s, but the family came out ahead in the end. As one of its sales come-ons, Britannica sponsored essay contests for its customers' children. Young Michael and his three sisters racked up $2,500 in essay prize money, and won four complete sets of the Great Books for their high school. In the end, he lost interest in the set, which "invited worship rather than discussion. . . . Not the sort of books one reads under the cover with a flashlight," Dirda concluded.

It *is* hard to resist poking fun. And yet. About two-thirds of the way through my research, I found myself occasionally succumbing to creeping Great Books-ism, almost like a low-level staph infection that invaded my metabolism. When my local library reading group assigned Aristophanes's *Lysistrata*, I embarked on what my mother would call a "jag" ("Oh, you're on a Greek 'jag'"), reading three or four of the playwright's hilarious, bawdy, wildly disjointed and awfully translated plays in a row. On a whim, I picked up a copy of John Stuart Mill's autobiography, the book that convinced Mortimer Adler that he was wasting his time scribbling for the *New York Sun*, and prompted him to apply to Columbia. It did not convince me to stop scribbling for a living, but I read most of it, and enjoyed what I read. Adler seized on Mill's astonishing education, but I was seduced by Mill's Zen-like conclusion that erudition can't buy you love or, in his case, happiness: "Those only are happy," Mill wrote, "who have their minds fixed on some object other than their own happiness."

Because the Columbia University bookstore places Epictetus's "Handbook" so near the cash registers, I spent a New York to

Boston train ride feasting on the delightful first-century philosopher whose thoughts undergirded Tom Wolfe's sprawling 1998 best-seller, *A Man in Full*. I fell in love with the gnarly-legged Stoic when he wrote: "If you drink water, do not say at every opening that you drink water." It was as if he had read my mind. At the time I had forsworn alcohol, and made a great show of carrying my own bottles of Pellegrino or Perrier to dinner parties. He had pricked the vanity of my preening abstemiousness. "If you wish to train yourself to hardship," he wrote, "do it for yourself and not for those outside." Another line of his that I love: "Remember that the contest is *now*, the Olympic games are *now*, and you cannot put things off anymore." I remember.

In the first chapter, I noted that early-to-the-game bookies likes Frederic Farrar and Auguste Comte believed in literary "hygiene," that a taste for good books chased out a taste for the bad. They are right; greatness can spoil one's appetite for the merely normal. This happened to me. After leaving my Chicago Great Books weekend, where about a hundred of us discussed not only Swift but also *Oedipus Rex* and Sherwood Anderson's *Winesburg, Ohio*, I was pining for an un-Great book. At O'Hare airport, I snatched John Hart's sexed-up legal thriller *The King of Lies* off a paperback rack. For about the ten-thousandth time, I bought a book for its cover. I read it, and I hated it. It was one of the worst books I have ever read. Curse you, Sophocles! Curse you, Sherwood Anderson!

Both Adler and Hutchins died deeply disappointed men. They were convinced that they had an important message for the world, and the world spurned them. Or did it? How far removed is Oprah's Book Club, headquartered in Chicago just a few miles from Adler's old offices, from the better-living-through-reading precepts of the Great Bookies? In 2004, Oprah helped sell a million copies of Tolstoy's *Anna Karenina*, a great book by almost any definition. What is the Teaching Company, which flogs its Great Courses DVDs in the *Wall Street Journal*, the *New York Times*, and elsewhere, if not a digital version of the Great Books? "Park your car in Harvard yard?" a Teaching Company ad asks, channeling the bygone hucksters of Chicago's Midway. "No, it's more like parking Harvard in your car, living room, and life!"

What is the "One Day University," which packages lectures by professors from Harvard, Yale, Princeton, and Columbia into a daylong Chautauqua format, if not a come-hither marketing scheme reminiscent of the Britannica hucksters? "There is an illusion that Americans wanted it then and don't want it now," says Peter Temes, the former Great Books Foundation president who now organizes Great Books seminars for business executives and aspirational high school students. "Homer, Plato, Socrates, Emily Dickinson, Cervantes—what an inspiring list of great writers, and what a challenge for young and old alike to pick up these works and make them new," reads the hype for Temes's Great Books Summer Program. "Our approach to sparking dialogue dates back to Plato's teacher Socrates."

The Great Books are out there, to be sure. A Massachusetts psychiatrist, Jonathan Shay, won a MacArthur "genius" grant for his work teaching *The Iliad* and *The Odyssey* to traumatized war veterans. Educator Earl Shorris, who likes to quote Robert Hutchins's dictum that "the best education for the best is the best education for all," started teaching the Great Books at the Roberto Clemente Family Guidance Center in Manhattan in 1997. Now administered by Bard College, the Clemente program has been tried in fourteen states. Three St. John's College tutors first introduced their Socratic, Great Books seminar pedagogy, called Touchstones, into an inner-city magnet school in Hartford,

Connecticut, in 1985. Over 500,000 men and women have since participated in Touchstones discussion groups, in school systems around the world, in prisons, at the National Security Agency, and at the Austen Riggs mental hospital in western Massachusetts. Even though Touchstones uses the texts of Plato, Aquinas, and other ancients, the phrase *Great Books* does not appear in any of their materials. Cofounder Howard Zeiderman says Touchstones has modified, and improved upon, the "shared inquiry" model. "I don't call it Great Books because that focuses on the text as a kind of artifact or museum piece," he says, "rather than on the experience of the people in the discussion. Our model is a kind of pilgrimage for the group; I am trying to turn leadership over to them. That would be heretical on other programs."

While it would be a wild exaggeration to suggest that the Great Books are making a comeback in the academy, the situation certainly isn't as glum as Yale's professionally despondent Harold Bloom wrote in *The Western Canon* in 1994: "Things . . . have fallen apart, the center has not held, and mere anarchy is in the process of being unleashed upon what used to be called 'the learned world.'" It is true that one would be hard-pressed to find "general education" requirements, or obligatory Western Civilization curricula, at most universities. There are, however, several modest programs that have puttered forward during the past decades, most of them inspired by Hutchins's and Adler's Chicago experiments. Tiny Shimer College has been teaching a Great Books curriculum since the Hutchins era, occasionally teetering on the verge of oblivion. Small Catholic institutions like Thomas Aquinas College and St. Mary's College, both in California, teach the Great Books. Notre Dame's three-year Program of Liberal Studies has been teaching Great Books seminars since 1950, a product of Adler's friendship with the university's former president, John Cavanaugh. The program once had 160 students, but now, competing with electives, double majors, and junior years abroad, it has about 120. "We face a challenge in recruiting that we didn't have in the past," chairman Stephen Fallon says.

Even Yale ("supine before oncoming waves of multiculturalists," Bloom groaned) offers a one-year-long Great Books program, called Directed Studies, to about 10 percent of its freshmen each year. In the late 1990s, *after* both Blooms decried the disappearance of the Great Books, DS increased its enrollment from 90 to its current level of 125, says program director Jane Levin: "It's very popular." I noticed that a recent DS syllabus included only one woman, Hannah Arendt, among the fifty authors being studied. Had any undergraduates complained about the overrepresentation of the old, bearded fellows on the course list, I asked? "Truthfully? No, they haven't," she replied.

Every ten years or so, a popular writer rediscovers the Western tradition. In 1987, Allan Bloom proclaimed his love for the great, classical works: "The books in their objective beauty are still there," he wrote, "and we must protect and cultivate the delicate tendrils reaching out toward them through the unfriendly soil of students' souls." In 1997, at the end of his "adventures with Homer, Rousseau, Woolf and other indestructible writers of the Western World," the *New Yorker*'s David Denby concluded that "the culture-ideologues, both left and right, are largely talking nonsense." "The great thing about Western culture," he wrote, "is that any American can stand on it, or on some small part of it. . . . The courses in the Western classics force us to ask all those questions about self and society we no longer address without embarrassment—the questions our media-trained habits of irony have tricked us out of asking."

In 2007, Yale's Anthony Kronman reported in his book *Education's End: Why Our Colleges and Universities Have Given Up on the Meaning of Life* that "the excitement that accompanied the ideas of multiculturalism and constructivism in their early days has subsided." A former dean of the Yale Law School—shades of Robert Hutchins!—Kronman boldly opined that "it is not only appropriate but necessary to speak of the privileged position of Western civilization,"

> understanding by this the unique place which the civilization that began in the West but now rests on universal moral and intellectual foundations occupies among the civilizations of the world. The ideas and institutions of the West, liberated from the accidental limits of their historical beginnings, have become the common possession of humanity.

For the past several years, Kronman has been teaching in Yale's Directed Studies program. "At the heart of the program is the question of what living is for," he writes. Who is on the reading list? If you don't know by now, then you haven't been paying attention: Plato, Aristotle, Epictetus, Herodotus, Thucydides, Aquinas, Augustine, Descartes, Dante, Shakespeare, Flaubert, Goethe, Milton, Locke, Rousseau, Machiavelli, and Mill. It is funny how their names keep coming up.

Really. Have you ever had that experience, when you learn someone's name, and suddenly you start seeing it all the time? Sometimes I feel as if I am surrounded by Great Books. At an achingly cutesy chocolatier in the old mill town of Pittsfield,

Massachusetts, friends told me about businessman Robert Strassler, who has commissioned opulent new coffee-table editions of Herodotus and Thucydides. A *New Yorker* review of the Strassler Herodotus declared, without irony, that "the father of lies" was *hot*: "The moment has come, once again, for Herodotus' dazzlingly associative style."

While writing these pages, I bought Michael Harvey's shoot-em-up detective novel *The Chicago Way*, "steeped in the glorious, gritty atmosphere of a great city," to learn more about Chicago. What did I get? Several lines rendered in ancient Greek, including the famous aphorism γνωθι σεαυτόν ("know thyself") inscribed on the wall of the oracle at Delphi. Harvey was a classics major in college. In James Collins's recently published romantic novel *Beginner's Greek*, the boy-girl intrigue hatches from a shared love of Thomas Mann's *The Magic Mountain*, which the beautiful Holly is reading on a New York to Los Angeles flight. The male lead Peter, an icon of eligibility traced from the Jane Austen template, is reading Charles Dickens's *David Copperfield*.

They are everywhere!

The Great Books are dead. Long live the Great Books!

ACKNOWLEDGMENTS

W RITING IS TRAVELING, even if you never leave your room. So many people helped me on this journey; here is my chance to thank them.

My longtime friend and literary agent Michael Carlisle always liked this project. His father, the writer Henry Carlisle, had a whiff of the Robert Hutchins magic as a young man. When I proposed writing about this abstruse, fundamentally Midwestern topic, Michael encouraged me. Editors Lisa Kaufman and Susan Weinberg at PublicAffairs books were equally enthusiastic. For her sins, Lisa had to edit the manuscript, and of course did an excellent job. Thank you to all.

There may come a time when newspaper writers won't be able to thank their colleagues for book help, because daily print journalism is heading the way of, well, the Great Books. Happily, that time is not now, so I can thank my editors at the *Boston Globe*—Martin Baron, Fiona Luis, Mary Jane Wilkinson, and Stephen Greenlee—for freeing me to work on this project. Mark Feeney and David Warsh laughed when they heard my title; I took that as a good sign. Wesley Morris loaned me the Great

Books he read as a boy. Lisa Tuite and her talented research team at the *Boston Globe* library—Richard Pennington, Elizabeth Grillo, Marleen Lee, Marc Shechtman, Matthew Mahoney, Robert Burke, Rosemary McDonald, Jeremiah Manion, and Colneth Smiley—helped me early and often.

I believe that librarians are the unacknowledged legislators of the universe. The past three years have only confirmed my view. At the University of Chicago's Special Collections Research Center, Julia Gardner, Christine Colburn, and Judith Dartt were especially helpful. At Harvard, Barbara Meloni and Tim Driscoll offered me aid, as did *Harvard* magazine editors John Rosenberg and Jennifer Carling. Job-sharing Stanford librarians Michelle Futornick and Regina Kammer found materials for me. I also received help from Columbia's Rare Book and Manuscript Library, and from my wonderful public library in Newton, Massachusetts. At the Federal Trade Commission, Jackie Dizdul chased down materials for me. As did Audrey Fischer at the Library of Congress, and Edward C. Fields and Jennifer Mundy Johnson at the University of California, Santa Barbara.

In Chicago, many people were generous with their advice and company. Historian Tim Lacy not only squired me to Mike Royko's old hangout, The Billy Goat Tavern, but also gave me a digital version of his excellent PhD on the Great Books. At the University of Chicago, Josh Schonwald helped me with many questions, as did students Luke Joyner and Tim Murphy. I learned a great deal from Dean John Boyer, and from Professors Michael Jones, James Chandler, Francisco Barrenechea, and Steven Walt, who is now at Harvard. Thank you, Clare Pearson, for teaching me about the Basic Program. At the Great Books Foundation, Daniel Born, Don Whitfield, George Schueppert, Carolyn Groenewold, Jason Smith, and Susan Hayes offered me invaluable aid. Tom Panelas answered my questions about Britannica. In Massachusetts, Vincent Stanton, Ruth Greene, and Peg Mahoney helped me enjoy my local Great Books reading group.

Special thanks to ur-Chicagoans Max Weissmann of the Center for the Study of The Great Ideas, and Sydney Hyman, for their time and help.

At St. John's College, the legendary tutor Eva Brann put me in touch with Dean Michael Dink, who arranged for my visit. I enjoyed speaking with tutors Leo Pickens, Susan Paalman, Emily Rena-Dozier, Nick Maistrellis, and Howard Zeiderman. Students Erica Beall, Clint Richardson, John Okrent, Paul Wilford, and Molly Rothenberg were kind enough to spend time with me. Communications director Rosemary Harty generously provided me with background materials.

Michael Holquist, Jonathon Kahn, John Battat, Addison Anderson, Rebecca Lee, Roosevelt Montas, Christopher Beam, and Michael Shavelson helped me navigate the nuances of Columbia's core curricula. Dorie Baker, Jane Levin, and Penelope Laurans explained Yale's Directed Studies program to me. Matt Storin and Stephen Fallon introduced me to Notre Dame's Program of Liberal Studies.

Thanks to Peter Temes, who continues to be involved with Great Books, and to John Kristensen of the Firefly Press, who explained Fairfield type. Mark Adler graciously spent the better part of a hot Washington, D.C., day with me, talking about his father. Karen Pizarro, Tom Hyland, Jr., Ralph Whitehead, Jr., the late Rhoda Pritzker, Sue Lummis, and Michael Dirda were kind enough to discuss their Great Books experiences with me.

This is the second book I have published with PublicAffairs. All writers should be so lucky. I have already mentioned Lisa and Susan. I also enjoyed counsel from Clive Priddle, Whitney Peeling, and Peter Osnos. PublicAffairs turned my manuscript over to a formidable, University of Chicago–educated production team. Thank you, Meredith Smith and Christine Arden, for wrestling my book into shape.

"Better a hundred friends than a hundred rubles," the Russians say. I don't have a hundred friends, but I treasure the ones I have. Thank you Richard Roecklein, Margaret Ferguson, Eric Tomb, Byron Swift, and Margo Howard for your help. My mother remains a great friend and a sharp-eyed one at that; thanks for spotting the Susan Sontag material, Mom. A friend can make no greater sacrifice than to read a manuscript, and Katherine Powers and Cullen Murphy read parts of this one. My wife Kirsten Lundberg, one of the best writers I know, read the entire manuscript and made many important suggestions. I claim—nay, embrace—this book's shortcomings as my own.

THE (RANDOMLY ANNOTATED) GREAT BOOKS OF THE WESTERN WORLD

CHOSEN BY MORTIMER J. ADLER, ROBERT M. HUTCHINS & CO.

HUTCHINS: *"He did the work, I took the credit."*

1. Homer: *The Iliad* and *The Odyssey*

    "The greatest adventure story of all time"

    —HUTCHINS

2. Aeschylus, seven plays; Sophocles, the Oedipus cycle plus three plays; Euripides, nineteen plays; Aristophanes, eleven plays

    The U.S. Postmaster General declared Aristophanes's *Lysistrata* to be obscene, creating problems for the Great Books Foundation in 1955.

3. Herodotus: *The History*

    The best account of the 300 Spartans' stand at Thermopylae.

4. Thucydides: *The History of the Peloponnesian War*

    Boasts of "no fables," contrasting his work with that of Herodotus.

5.   Plato: *The Republic* and twenty-four other works

> "There you are," said Alcibiades, "just as usual: when Socrates is present, nobody else has a chance with the handsome ones. You see how resourceful he was in devising a plausible reason why our young friend should sit beside him."

6.   Aristotle, two volumes: thirty-one works, including *Rhetoric, Politics, The Nichomachean Ethics, On Sleep and Sleeplessness*

> "Poppy, mandragora, wine, darnel, produce a heaviness in the head."

7.   Hippocrates: seventeen works, including *The Oath, On Fistulae, On Hemorrhoids*

> "Make the irons red-hot, and burn the pile until it be dried up, so as that no part may be left behind."

8.   Galen: *On the Natural Faculties*

> "Now Nature constructs bone, cartilage, nerve, membrane, ligament, vein, and so forth, at the first stage of the animal's genesis."

9.   Euclid: *The Elements*

> "FG, GH are rational straight lines commensurable in square only; therefore FH is an apotome. I say next that it is also a sixth apotome."

10. Archimedes: ten works, including the *Books of Lemmas, on the Sphere and Cylinder*

> Of the top ten, only Hippocrates and Archimedes did not appear on the committee's original, unanimous "first string" list.

11. Apollonius of Perga: *On Conic Sections*

> Omitted in the 1990 relaunch. "I regretted dropping the
> *Conics*," Adler lamented.

12. Nicomachus of Gerasa: *Introduction to Arithmetic*

> "The multiple superpartients and superpartients of other kinds
> are made to appear—out of the superpartients."

13. Lucretius: *On the Nature of Things*

> *I know how hard it is in Latin verse*
> *To tell the dark discoveries of the Greeks*

14. Epictetus: *The Discourses*

> "Men are disturbed, not by things, but by their own notions
> regarding them."

15. Marcus Aurelius: *The Meditations*

> "Highly teachable, but no real content," said selection
> committee member Joseph Schwab.

16. Virgil: *The Aeneid, The Eclogues, The Georgics*

> "A joy it will be one day, perhaps, to remember even this."

17. Plutarch: *The Lives*

> On Alexander the Great: "He was much less addicted to wine
> than was generally believed."

18. Tacitus: *The Annals, The Histories*

> "For when she consulted the astrologers about Nero,
> they replied that he would be emperor and kill his
> mother. 'Let him kill her,' she said, 'provided he
> is emperor.'"

19. Ptolemy: *The Almagest*

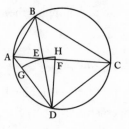

20. Copernicus: *On the Revolution of the Heavenly Spheres*

"We therefore assert that the center of the Earth, carrying the Moon's path, passes in a great circuit among the other planets in an annual revolution round the Sun; that near the Sun is the center of the Universe."

21. Kepler: *Epitome of Copernican Astronomy, The Harmonies of the World*

As a young man, Mark Adler, Mortimer's oldest son, read Kepler for fun: "I was curious. I wanted to learn about the music of the spheres."

22. Plotinus: *The Six Enneads*

"The sensitive principle is our scout; the Intellectual-Principle our King."

23. St. Augustine: *The Confessions, The City of God, On Christian Doctrine*

"But what were the causes for my strong dislike of Greek literature, which I studied from my boyhood?"

24. St. Thomas Aquinas, two volumes: *Summa Theologica*

Omitted from the Harvard Classics.

25. Dante Alighieri: *The Divine Comedy*

> *O people whose sharp fervor now perhaps*
> *Redeems the negligence and dallying*
> *You showed in lukewarmness for doing good*

26. Geoffrey Chaucer: *Troilus and Cressida, The Canterbury Tales*

> *Criseyde was this lady name a-right;*
> *As to my dome, in al Troyes citee*
> *Nas noon so fair, for passing every wight*
> *So aungellyk was hir natyf beautee*

27. Machiavelli: *The Prince*

> "Princes should have anything blamable administered by others, favors by themselves."

28. Thomas Hobbes: *Leviathan*

> "What a grim and dislikable writer! Yet how hard he is to shake off!"
>
> —DAVID DENBY

29. Francois Rabelais: *Gargantua and Pantagruel*

> "Rabelais' *Gargantua* was never a great book, it was condemned by the Sorbonne when it was first written and the vulgar of the world have dragged it down its dirty path to this day."
>
> —LETTER FROM A DISAFFECTED GREAT BOOKS GROUP MEMBER
> TO HUTCHINS, 1950

30. Montaigne: *Essays*

> "Montaigne is not what the world needs"
>
> —HUTCHINS

31. Shakespeare, two volumes: thirty-eight plays and *The Sonnets*

> "Shakespeare and Dante are the Western canon"
>
> —HAROLD BLOOM

32. William Gilbert: *On the Loadstone and Magnetic Bodies*

> "The ingenious Fracastorio, a distinguished philosopher, in seeking the reason for the direction of the loadstone, feigns Hyperborean magnetick mountains attracting magnetical things of iron."

33. Galileo: *Dialogues Concerning the Two New Sciences*

> "It is clear that Aristotle could not have made the experiment; yet he wishes to give us the impression of his having performed it."

34. William Harvey: three works, including *On the Circulation of the Blood*

> "If a live snake be laid open, the heart will be seen pulsating quietly, distinctly, for more than an hour, moving like a worm."

35. Cervantes: *Don Quixote*

> "Know, friend Sancho," said Don Quixote, "that the life of knights-errant is subject to a thousand dangers and reverses."

36. Sir Francis Bacon: three works, including *The New Atlantis*

> "Know, therefore, that with them there are no stews, no dissolute houses, no courtesans, nor anything of that kind. Nay, they wonder, with detestation, at you in Europe, which permit such things."

37. Descartes: five works, including *The Geometry*

> "I have never met with a single critic of my opinions who did not appear to me either less rigorous or less equitable than myself."

38. Milton: four works, including *Paradise Lost*

> Robert Hutchins once remarked that one of the two titles he
> would have chosen for an autobiography was "Natural Tears,"
> an allusion to Adam and Eve's reaction to their expulsion from
> Paradise: "Some natural tears they dropped, but wiped them
> soon; The world was all before them."

39. Pascal: nine works, including *Les Pensées*

> "Man is neither angel nor brute, and the unfortunate thing is
> that he who would act the angel acts the brute."

40. Newton: *Mathematical Principles of Natural Philosophy*,
    Optics

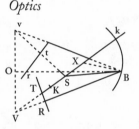

41. Christian Huygens: *Treatise on Light*

> See my introduction

42. John Locke: four works, including *An Essay Concerning
    Human Understanding*

> "Notwithstanding these learned disputants, these all-
> knowing doctors, it was to the unscholastic statesman that
> the governments of the world owed their peace, defence, and
> liberties; and from the illiterate and contemned mechanic (a
> name of disgrace) that they received the improvements of
> useful arts."

43. George Berkeley: *The Principles of Human Knowledge*

> "Apodictically I would declare that Berkeley's *Principles of Human Knowledge* is a classic."
>
> —ADLER

44. David Hume: *An Enquiry Concerning Human Understanding*

> "An old ass" —HUTCHINS

45. Jonathan Swift: *Gulliver's Travels*

> "Several of this cursed Brood getting hold of the Branches behind, leaped up in the Tree, from whence they began to discharge their Excrements on my Head."

46. Laurence Sterne: *Tristram Shandy*

> The only book that Hutchins insisted be included. It amused him. It was dropped from the 1990 edition, after his death.

47. Henry Fielding: *Tom Jones*

> Also dumped in 1990. "I thought we were wrong in dropping Fielding," Adler lamented, again.

48. Montesquieu: *The Spirit of Laws*

> "[Alexander] committed two very bad actions in setting Persepolis on fire and slaying Clitus; but he rendered them famous by his repentance. Hence it is that his crimes are forgotten, while his regard for virtue was recorded."

49. Rousseau: three works, including *The Social Contract*

> "If Sparta and Rome perished, what State can hope to endure for ever?"

50. Adam Smith: *The Wealth of Nations*

> "But though North America is not yet so rich as England, it is
> much more thriving, and advancing with much greater rapidity
> to the further acquisition of riches."

51. Edward Gibbon, two volumes: *The Decline and Fall of the
Roman Empire*

> "During the age of Christ . . . the doctrine which they preached
> was confirmed by innumerable prodigies. The lame walked,
> the blind saw, the sick were healed, the dead were raised,
> daemons were expelled, and the laws of Nature were frequently
> suspended for the benefit of the church."

52. Immanuel Kant: seven works, including *The Critique of
Pure Reason*

> "To know what questions may reasonably be asked is already a
> great and necessary proof of sagacity and insight."

53. American State Papers: including *The Declaration of
Independence* and *The Constitution*

> "When in the course of human events," etc.

54. Alexander Hamilton, John Madison, and John Jay:
The Federalist Papers

> "I go further, and affirm that bills of rights, in the sense and in the
> extent in which they are contended for, are not only unnecessary
> in the proposed constitution, but would even be dangerous."

55. John Stuart Mill: three works, including *On Liberty*

> But not the *Autobiography*, the book that prompted Adler to
> ditch journalism for Plato

56. James Boswell: *The Life of Johnson*

> My idea of a great book.

57. Antoine Lavoisier: *Elements of Chemistry*

> "In those days, without possessing facts, they framed systems; while we, who have collected facts, seem determined to reject even these, when they do not agree with our prejudices."

58. Jean Baptiste Fourier: *Theory of Heat*

> Eliminated in 1990

59. Michael Faraday: *Experimental Research in Electricity*

> "If the wire—p'n'—be carried up from below, it will pass in the opposite direction between the magnetic poles; but then also the magnetic poles themselves are reversed."

60. Hegel: *The Philosophy of Right*, *The Philosophy of History*

> "Spirit does not toss itself about in the external play of chance occurrences; on the contrary, it is that which determines history absolutely, and it stands firm against the chance occurrences which it dominates and exploits for its own purpose."

61. Goethe: *Faust*

> *Methinks, by most, 'twill be confess'd*
> *That Death is never quite a welcome guest.*

62. Melville: *Moby-Dick*

> Attempted blackballing ("if Whitman goes, Melville goes") by Great Books progenitor John Erskine failed.

63. Darwin: *The Origin of Species, The Descent of Man*

> "Many kinds of monkeys have a strong taste for tea, coffee, and spirituous liquors; they will also, as I have myself seen, smoke tobacco with pleasure."

64. Marx and Marx and Engels: *Capital, The Communist Manifesto*

> "The fate of humanity depends on the ability of Christians to demonstrate, by words and deeds, the fallacy of this 'great book.'"
>
> —THE GREAT BOOKS: A CHRISTIAN APPRAISAL

65. Tolstoy: *War and Peace*

> "'But every time there have been conquests there have been conquerors; every time there has been a revolution in any state there have been great men,' says history."

66. Dostoevsky: *The Brothers Karamazov*

> "'Stay, stay,' laughed Ivan. 'how hot you are! A fantasy you say, let it be so! Of course it's a fantasy. But allow me to say: do you really think that the Roman Catholic movement of the last centuries is actually nothing but the lust of power, of filthy earthly gain?'"

67. William James: *The Principles of Psychology*

> "We are sure that fire will burn and water wet us, less sure that thunder will come after lightning, not at all sure whether a strange dog will bark at us or let us go by. In these ways experience moulds us every hour, and makes of our minds a mirror of the time- and space-connections between the things in the world."

68. Sigmund Freud: eighteen works, including *The Interpretation of Dreams, On Narcissism*

> In his 1940 bestseller *How to Read a Book*, Adler consigned Freud to a subsidiary list of "good, but not great" writers. Among great writers, he included Henry Thomas Buckle and Charles Lyell.

ADDED IN 1990:

69. John Calvin: *Institutes of the Christian Religion*

> "We have a frenzied desire, an infinite eagerness, to pursue wealth and honour, intrigue for power, accumulate riches, and collect all those frivolities which seem conducive to luxury and splendor."

70. Erasmus: *The Praise of Folly*

> "*The Praise of Folly* is famous by its title but it seems to me a pretty dead work." —JOHN ERSKINE

71. Molière: seven plays

> "Molière will go out only over my bruised body," Mark Van Doren said during the first round of selections. "It's trash, professor, and nothing else."
> —HUTCHINS TO ADLER RE: MOLIÈRE

72. Jean Racine: two plays

> Andromache: "Can I forget Hector unburied, dragged in dishonor round our walls? Can I forget his father thrown down at my feet, covering the altar with blood?"

73. Voltaire: *Candide*

> "The single most influential figure of the eighteenth century," according to Hutchins, who couldn't jawbone the Frenchman into Round One.

74. Diderot: *Rameau's Nephew*

> "If I understood history, I'd show you that evil has always come here below from some man of genius."

75. Kierkegaard: *Fear and Trembling*

> "When the child has grown and is to be weaned, the mother virginally covers her breast, so the child no more has a mother. Lucky the child that lost its mother in no other way!"

76. Nietzsche: *Beyond Good and Evil*

> "A thing explained is a thing we have no further concern with.—What did that god mean who counselled: 'know thyself!'?Does that perhaps mean: 'Have no further concern with thyself! become objective!'"

77. Toqueville: *Democracy in America*

> "So many lucky men, restless in the midst of abundance."

78. Balzac: *Cousin Bette*

> "'If you save my life,' she asked, 'shall I be as good-looking as ever? 'Possibly,' said the physician, slowly.
> 'I know your "possibly," said Valerie. 'I shall look like a woman who has fallen into the fire! No! Leave me to the Church. I can please no one now but God.'"

79. Jane Austen: *Emma*

> "It darted through her with the speed of an arrow that Mr. Knightley must marry no one but herself!"

80. George Eliot: *Middlemarch*

> "We have come a long way, baby," read the promotional teaser, "and thus we have Jane and George, as well as Willa Cather and Virginia Woolf in the 20th century."

81. Charles Dickens: *Little Dorrit*
    Finally

82. Mark Twain: *Huckleberry Finn*
    Finally

83. Henrik Ibsen: four plays

84. In one volume: essays by William James ("Pragmatism); Henri Bergson ("An Introduction to Metaphysics"); John Dewey ("Experience and Education"); Alfred North Whitehead ("Science and the Modern World"); Bertrand Russell ("The Problems of Philosophy"); Martin Heidegger ("What Is Metaphysics?"); Ludwig Wittgenstein ("Philosophical Investigations"); Karl Barth ("The Word of God and The Word of Man")

85. In one volume: essays by Henri Poincare ("Science and Hypothesis"); Max Planck ("Scientific Autobiography"); Whitehead ("An Introduction to Mathematics"); Albert Einstein ("Relativity"); Arthur Eddington ("The Expanding Universe"); Niels Bohr ("Selections"); G. H. Hardy ("A Mathematician's Apology"); Werner Heisenberg ("Physics and Philosophy"); Erwin Schrodinger ("What Is Life?"); Theodosius Dobzhansky ("Genetics and the Origin of Species"); C. H. Waddington ("The Nature of Life")

86. In one volume: Thorstein Veblen (*The Theory of the Leisure Class*); R. H. Tawney (*The Acquisitive Society*); J. M. Keynes (*The General Theory*)

87. In one volume: James Frazer (*Golden Bough*, selections); Max Weber (*Essays in Sociology*, selections); Johan Huizinga (*The Waning of the Middle Ages*); Claude Levi-Strauss (*Structural Anthropology*, selections)

88. In one volume: Henry James (*The Beast in the Jungle*); G. B. Shaw (*Saint Joan*); Joseph Conrad (*Heart of Darkness*); Anton Chekhov (*Uncle Vanya*); Luigi Pirandello (*Six Characters in Search of an Author*); Marcel Proust (*Swann in Love*); Willa Cather (*A Lost Lady*); Thomas Mann (*A Death in Venice*); James Joyce (*A Portrait of the Artist*)

89. In one volume: Virginia Woolf (*To the Lighthouse*); Franz Kafka (*Metamorphosis*); D. H. Lawrence (*The Prussian Officer*); T. S. Eliot (*The Waste Land*); Eugene O'Neill (*Mourning Becomes Electra*); F. Scott Fitzgerald (*The Great Gatsby*); William Faulkner (*A Rose for Emily*); Bertolt Brecht (*Mother Courage*); Ernest Hemingway (*The Short Happy Life of Francis Macomber*); George Orwell (*Animal Farm*); Samuel Beckett (*Waiting for Godot*)

In the final six volumes Adler & Co. did precisely what they had earlier reviled the Harvard Classics for doing—that is, printing short works and excerpts by famous writers and thinkers.

NOTES ON SOURCES

There have been three thoroughly researched dissertations written on the Great Books movement, all of which were very valuable to me. They are: Hugh Moorhead's 1964 thesis, "The Great Books Movement"; Amy Apfel Kass's "Radical Conservatives for Liberal Education," completed in 1973; and Tim Lacy's 2006 dissertation, "Making a Democratic Culture: The Great Books Idea, Mortimer J. Adler, and Twentieth-Century America."

All three scholars mined the key archives at the University of Chicago and elsewhere before I did, and following their work eased my own research burden considerably. In many cases, all four of us perused the same documents and excerpted exactly the same comments and quotations. They showed me the way.

Although I cite some smaller collections below, the main archives for any study of the Great Books are to be found in the Special Collections Research Center at the University of Chicago's Regenstein Library. The Robert Hutchins, William Benton, and Mortimer Adler papers are open and available to the public.

ONE: THE HEADWATERS

I was helped in this section by W. B. Carnochan's useful and amusing overview, "Where Did Great Books Come From, Anyway?" published in the *Stanford Humanities Review* in 1998. Equally valuable was Adam Kirsch's *Harvard* magazine article on the "five-foot shelf," "Eliot's Elect: The Harvard Classics, 1910," published in 2001.

For information on Charles Eliot, and the Harvard and Yale curricula before and after his reforms, I used Samuel Eliot Morrison's 1936 classic, *Three Centuries of Harvard*, and Volume 1 of Yale's rival text, *Yale: College and University*, by George Pierson, published in 1952. I also consulted John Bethell's lively and readable illustrated history, *Harvard Observed*, from 1998.

I met Hannah Gray at a Great Books conference at Yale in 2006.

Adler writes about his early years in the first of his two autobiographies, *A Philosopher at Large*.

John Erskine also wrote several books about himself, including *The Memory of Certain Persons* and *My Life as a Teacher*, in which he mentions his attempts to launch General Honors at Columbia. Two Columbia books, Ashbel Green's 2004 *My Columbia: Reminiscences of University Life* and *Living Legacies at Columbia*, edited in 2006 by William Theodore de Bary, have lots of information about the Erskine seminar. Joan Shelley Rubin devotes a chapter to Erskine in her 1992 book, *The Making of Middlebrow Culture*. I also spent some time at the modest John Erskine archive at Columbia's Butler Library.

Hugh Moorhead's dissertation has a useful account of the People's Institute. I found Adler's class notes at the Institute archive in the New York Public Library.

TWO: THE ODD COUPLE

There is a wealth of material on Hutchins and Adler. Hutchins has had several biographers, and Adler lived so long that he wrote two autobiographies. My favorite Hutchins biography is William McNeill's concise and stylish *Hutchins' University: A Memoir of the University of Chicago 1929–1950*. Harry Ashmore's 1989 *Unseasonable Truths: The Life of Robert Maynard Hutchins* is also invaluable, and Milton Mayer's energetic and opinionated *Robert Maynard Hutchins: A Memoir* is required reading. Mary Ann Dzuback's 1991 book about Hutchins, *Robert M. Hutchins: Portrait of an Educator*, is helpful, thorough, and accurate.

Chicago dean John Boyer has published the definitive histories of the turbulent Hutchins era, in a series of monographs that are part of the University of Chicago's Occasional Papers on Higher Education.

My knowledge of John Dewey comes from Jay Martin's 2002 biography, *The Education of John Dewy*, and from Louis Menand's *The Metaphysical Club*, of 2001.

The note from Rhoda Pritzker was a personal communication. The Adler and Hutchins notes reproduced here are from the University of Chicago's presidential archive.

THREE: THE GREAT BOOKS IN THE GRAY CITY

Donald Miller's *City of the Century: The Epic of Chicago and the Making of America* provides a useful overview of the founding of the University of Chicago, and helped me distinguish the "White City" from the "Gray City" on the shores of Lake Michigan.

Katharine ("Kay") Graham recalled her Chicago undergraduate experience in her 1997 memoir, *Personal History*. The Susan Sontag quotations come from Molly McQuade's excellent *An Unsentimental Education: Writers and Chicago*, published in 1995. Joseph Epstein reminisced about Adler in "The Great Bookie," published in the *Weekly Standard* in 2001. Sydney Hyman's comments are based on our talks. George McElroy reminisced about the Adler-Hutchins Great Book course in the University of Chicago alumni magazine of August 2002.

The Saul Bellow quotations are from James Atlas's 2002 *Bellow: A Biography*, and from a lengthy 1984 interview in *TriQuarterly* magazine. The three above-mentioned dissertations all cover the issues in this chapter.

Time first put Robert Hutchins on its cover on June 24, 1935.

FOUR: GREAT BOOKS GOOD FOR YOU!

The three above-mentioned dissertations all cover the issues in this chapter, and the Great Books Foundation dug out back copies of its newsletter for me to peruse. Benjamin McArthur's long essay on the Great Books appeared in *American Heritage* magazine in 1989. Paul Mellon described his experiences with the Great Books in his 1992 memoir, *Reflections in a Silver Spoon*.

Joan Shelley Rubin's *The Making of Middlebrow Culture* is the definitive work on American "middlebrow."

James Sloan Allen tells the story of Walter Paepcke and the Aspen Institute in his excellent 1983 book, *The Romance of Commerce and Culture*.

The Liebling quote is from his 1952 *New Yorker* articles, "The Second City," reprinted as a paperback in 2004. I interviewed Julie Adams in 2008.

Timothy Cross's *An Oasis of Order: The Core Curriculum at Columbia College*, published in 1995 by the Office of the Dean, Columbia College, can be read on the Columbia University website.

FIVE: THE MAKING OF THE BOOKS

The biographical details about William Benton come from Sidney Hyman's 1969 biography, *The Lives of William Benton*, and from Joseph Epstein's 5,000-word review of Hyman's book, "Just Plain Bill," published in the *New York Review of Books* in 1970. Epstein also wrote a memorable, biting reminiscence of Hutchins, "The Sad Story of the Boy Wonder," in *Commentary* in 1990.

There are many sources for the memos that circulated during the Great Books selection process. I read the originals in the Adler and Hutchins archives. Hugh Moorhead and Tim Lacy quote extensively from the documents, and even the Great Books Foundation squirreled away their own set, which I also read. The Saul Bellow quote is from James Atlas's biography. Marshall McLuhan wrote about the Syntopicon in 1951, in *The Mechanical Bride*. Likewise, Joan Shelley Rubin casts a gimlet eye on the Syntopicon in *The Making of Middlebrow Culture*.

I have a copy of Hutchins and Adler's promotional film for the Great Books set, which I bought from Max Weismann's Center for the Study of The Great Ideas.

SIX: FASTER, PUSSYCAT! SELL! SELL!

Adler wrote extensively about his sales efforts in his first autobiography, and his Chicago archive is full of wild memos about sales strategies, etc. The deceptive sales techniques are detailed in two lengthy Federal Trade Commission documents, "In the Matter of Encyclopedia Britannica" Docket 7137, and the same title, Docket 8908. The Marplan report is in the Chicago archives, and Tim Lacy writes about it in his dissertation. Lacy also documents the many Great Books brand extensions.

I interviewed brothers Charles and John Van Doren, and exchanged e-mails with Michael Dirda, author of *An Open Book: Chapters from a Reader's Life*, 2004.

The *New York Times* covered Adler's Hickory Hill appearance, and my wife's cousin Eric Tomb sent me the wonderful Second City Great Books parody, which he preserved from his youth.

SEVEN: SECOND VERSE NOT THE SAME AS THE FIRST

Harry Ashmore's biography is the definitive source for the second half of Robert Hutchins's life. Hutchins appeared on *Time*'s cover for the second time on November 21, 1949.

The George Dell oral history interviews with both Adler and Hutchins are in the Regenstein Library, as are some of the Britannica marketing materials for the 1990 relaunch. Adler hailed the 1990 GBWW edition in his second autobiography, and the Library of Congress described the publication ceremony in its Information Bulletin.

EIGHT: THE PEOPLE OF THE BOOK

Great Books aficionado Ralph Whitehead and I had many talks and e-mail exchanges while I was writing this book.

Max Weismann was extremely generous with his time and sold me many of the materials I used to research this book. For instance, his Center for the Study of The Great Ideas has video recordings of every Mortimer Adler appearance on William F. Buckley's TV show *Firing Line* and copies of almost every article that Adler ever wrote. The Liebling quote is from his above-mentioned *New Yorker* articles.

Karen Hyland Pizarro and her brother Tom helped me enormously in assembling the story of their father's devotion to Great Books. They loaned me many different accounts of his World War II flying heroics, and other personal effects.

David Call was kind enough to spend time speaking with me on the telephone, and granted me permission to quote from his letters to Adler.

NINE: EPICTETUS AT THE CASH REGISTER

Most of the nation's major newspapers, including the *Chicago Tribune* and the *New York Times*, covered the Chicago "core wars," often re-working stories that first appeared in the university's student newspaper, the *Maroon*. Dean John Boyer and Humanities professor James Chandler granted me interviews, as did several Chicago students. Chandler's article on the core controversy appeared in the February 2001 issue of *University of Chicago Magazine*.

Columbia magazine editor Michael Shavelson provided me with invaluable background material about the university's core curricula, including magazine articles and the aforementioned books about the university.

Serendipitously, I learned that my friend Michael Holquist was teaching the core, and several teachers and students were also happy to discuss the program, including Jonathon Kahn, Roosevelt Montas, Jon Battat, Rebecca Lee, Christopher Beam, and others. The best-written modern account of the core is David Denby's *Great Books: My Adventures with Homer, Rousseau, Woolf, and Other Indestructible Writers of the Western World*, published in 1997. For facts and chronology, I relied on Timothy Cross's official history of the core.

TEN: HARD CORE

Amy Apfel Kass's PhD dissertation, cited above, has a valuable chapter on St. John's. Also helpful to me were Charles Nelson's "Radical Visions: Stringfellow Barr, Scott Buchanan, and Their Efforts on Behalf of Education and Politics in the Twentieth Century" (2001) and Nelson's "Stringfellow Barr: A Centennial Appreciation of His Life and Work" (1997).

A dated but very insightful appreciation of St. John's appeared in the 1978 book, *The Perpetual Dream: Reform and Experiment in the American College*, by Gerald Grant and David Riesman. I borrowed some of my historical background from that book. Eva Brann, Michael Dink, and Rosemary Harty were generous with their hospitality during my campus visit, allowing me to sit in on classes and meet students. Howard Zeiderman and Emily Rena-Dozier also talked to me about the colleges.

ELEVEN: AMONG THE BOOKIES

Daniel Born, Don Whitfield, and George Schueppert helped me get to know the Great Books Foundation. Born has written several perceptive essays on the history of the movement. Ruth Greene in Newton helped me join my local Great Books group, for which I am grateful.

TWELVE: DEAD BOOKS WALKING

The Allan Bloom quote comes from "The Closing of the American Mind," published in 1987, and Harold Bloom's remarks come from *The Western Canon*, which appeared in 1995. I interviewed Stephen Fallon, Howard Zeiderman, and Jane Levin.

INDEX